CAMRA'S
WILD
PUB WALKS

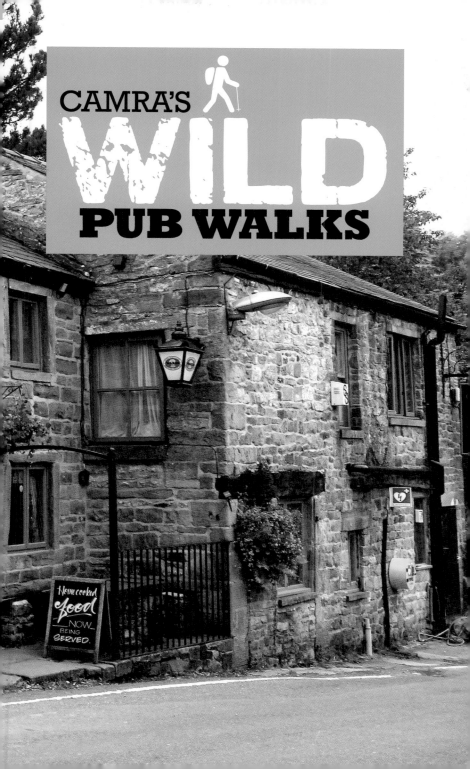

CAMRA'S WILD PUB WALKS

Published by the Campaign for Real Ale Ltd.
230 Hatfield Road
St Albans
Hertfordshire AL1 4LW
www.camra.org.uk/books

ISBN 978-1-85249-340-0

A CIP catalogue record for this book is available
from the British Library

Typeset in Rockwell and Myriad
Printed and bound in Wales by Cambrian Printers Ltd.

Head of Publishing: **Simon Hall**
Project Editors: **Katie Button, Julie Hudson**
Editorial Assistance: **Emma Haines**
Design and Cartography: **Stephen Bere**
Cover design: **Stephen Bere**
Design assistance: **Dale Tomlinson**
Senior Marketing Manager: **Chris Lewis**

contents

England 15

Scotland 93

Wales 141

Walk locator map

The walks in this guide have been grouped geographically into three sections. Walks 1–10 (orange) are in England: the Peak District, Lake District, Yorkshire Dales and North York Moors. Walks 11–17 (blue) are in Scotland: the Highlands and Borders. Walks 18–22 (purple) are in Wales: Snowdonia, the Brecon Beacons and Mid Wales.

Foreword by
Alan Hinkes OBE

It is a tradition among most hillwalkers and climbers to have a refreshing pint or two in the pub at the end of a strenuous day in the hills – some well-earned beer to celebrate a grand day out. What could be better for relaxing and bonding with your mates?

In the spring and summer months, after an energising fell walk one can often enjoy a long, pleasant evening outside in a beer garden. Although, in the summer I can often be outside on the hills and crags until after 10pm and then have to race down to the pub to catch last orders.

Sometimes in autumn and winter, when it's dark by 5pm in the northern fells, I go for a night walk. It's often on a snow-covered fell top on a clear moonlit night, when a head torch is hardly necessary. It's a good excuse to keep out of the pub on a long, cold evening. But I usually make sure I am back before closing time to enjoy a beer, prop up the bar or hunker around an open fire.

All of the routes in this book can be walked like this – as invigorating days in the outdoors with one or more good pubs at their end. I know most of the pubs that have been included and have done a lot of the walks in this book. And as well as recommending and advising Daniel on some of the routes, we have also tramped and scrambled some of them together, and supped a pint or two or more afterwards. Daniel and I are somewhat kindred spirits in our love of the hills and our passion for good beer – especially cask-conditioned ale, which is so much a part of the British pub's unique appeal.

My walking and climbing started in Yorkshire and Cumbria, progressing to the rest of the UK's mountains, the Alps and Himalaya. I've climbed Everest, K2 and many more, including all the fourteen 8,000-metre mountains; but I enjoy the British hills as much as any in the world, especially as there are no pubs in the Himalaya. (My 8,000-metre experiences are recounted in my book *8,000 Metres: Climbing The World's Highest Mountains.*)

Mind you, I have brewed beer at 5,200 metres in a Himalayan base camp, sampled beers in Kathmandu bars and drunk Chang – a Nepalese home-brew – in village shacks. All great experiences, but no substitute for a pint of cask-conditioned beer in a welcoming British pub.

Traditional walkers' refreshment

Real ale served in tip-top condition is a thing of beauty to be savoured. Some ales are subtle, thirst-quenching session beers; some modern brews are hoppy, spicy, flavour bombs. What I like is the depth of flavour and mellowness in a classic cask beer as well as the sheer variety of styles and flavours. Oh, and as well as quenching your thirst, beer has other benefits: It is somewhat isotonic; it contains yeast, vitamins (especially vitamin B), minerals (such as iron), carbohydrate and fluid (i.e. water). Oh, and alcohol – so don't drink too much.

This is a great and informative book to inspire you to get out there and walk in some fantastic areas of Britain. Enjoy the pubs and beer too, but stay sober for the next day's walk.

Alan Hinkes OBE

Introduction

Welcome to CAMRA's *Wild Pub Walks*, a walking guide that showcases the best of Britain's beautiful wild places, from the Brecon Beacons in south Wales to the Highlands of Scotland. Along with these upland and coastal walks, I have, of course, chosen some fantastic pubs serving well-kept real ales.

What is a wild pub walk?

Perhaps the best way to sum up my notion of a 'wild pub walk' and to give you a flavour of the sort of routes you will find in this book, is to describe my experience of one of the walks: that across Langdale Pikes in the Lake District (Walk 4)…

As my companion and I crossed the final stream and passed through the kissing gate, we could see the Old Dungeon Ghyll, our final destination for the day. We'd climbed up to Pavey Ark, high above Great Langdale in the Lake District, and across a few other tops. The weather was best described as 'dramatic'. Strong winds pushed the clouds across the sky at speed, opening up shafts of rich sunlight that focussed fleetingly across the impossibly green valleys. In the shadows, the giants of the Lake District loomed menacingly around us. In one moment we were drenched in a sharp shower and the next we were bathed in sunlight. The landscape never stood still, not for a second. Our route had taken us along a raging 'ghyll', up to a Lakeland tarn and, with a bit of hand placing, steeply up to our high point of the day, Harrison Stickle. Five hours or so later, we carried our excitement and exhilaration of this day (only slightly tempered by weary legs and cold toes) into the bar of the Old Dungeon Ghyll. A wood-burning stove raged along one wall. We ordered a different pint each and sat in front of the fire, our jackets steaming in front of it, and looked around. Everyone else in the bar was a walker, and they all had a similar look of contentment, joyously recounting the day and breaking into friendly banter. Another group of walkers joined us. We exchanged routes, bought rounds, remembered our favourite walks across Britain, and chatted on for a couple more hours. We had made new friends. We finally said goodbye and walked out into the cold night, with a warm glow inside us. It was the perfect mountain day, and one I wanted to replicate time and again with the walks in this book.

While in the planning stages of this book, I sat down with my friend Alan Hinkes, the only Brit to have climbed all fourteen 8,000-metre peaks. We'd met during my time editing hillwalking bible, *The Great Outdoors* magazine, and became friends over our mutual love of big British mountains and great British beer. We decided that the walks needed to take in some of the country's best scenery, whether that be up a vast Highland Munro, atop a remote Yorkshire moor, or along some dramatic coastline; and that there must be a couple of great pubs at the end of them. In short, the book needed to represent the kinds of days we enjoyed most and had shared a fair few of over the years. What follows are the walks we selected and I hope you enjoy them.

The walks

There are a huge variety of walks here, from remote Highland Munros to sea-swept walks along the Yorkshire Coast; from the uplands of south Wales to the always-exciting Kinder Scout in the Peak District. I've also included the highest mountain in England, in Wales and, the highest of them all, Ben Nevis in Scotland. I cover the safety aspects of the walks over pages 12–14, but many of the routes here take in high mountains and are best for experienced hillwalkers.

I also want to make clear that these walks are all designed to be done when there is no snow or ice on the ground. Walking in winter is an entirely different proposition and, for many of the walks in this book, the routes would become mountaineering expeditions.

I have graded the walks on a scale of fitness and navigation (from 1 to 4), bearing in mind that this book is designed for an outdoors enthusiast with experience in hillwalking. All are challenging from a fitness perspective as they mostly vary between 8 and 13 miles – plenty in anyone's book. When looking at the grading, also take into account not only the distance but, most importantly, the ascent. There are some big climbs in this book, and the difference between eight miles along the flat and eight miles over two mountains could be hours. Where possible, I've suggested shorter routes, but the nature of these walks means they can be quite committing.

Even more difficult to grade was navigation. On a sunny day with good visibility, most of the routes here should be fairly straightforward (for the sake of navigation, we stuck mainly to reasonably established paths), but when the cloud comes down, as it can do suddenly and at any time of year, navigation gets much, much more difficult, often requiring reliance upon a map and compass. I'll cover more aspects of this in the Safety First section but, suffice to say – these walks should only be attempted with a good understanding of how to use a map and compass. Purposely, I have not provided compass bearings, but I do constantly refer to grid references.

A final word of warning when deciding which walk to attempt: read through the entire description. There could be various places where a head for heights is required, or perhaps there's a hint of scrambling that inexperienced people could baulk at. An example is the Malham to Settle route that starts with a very short but committing scramble up the falls at Gordale Scar. I suggest an alternative route, but you don't want to get all the way there before realising that a member of your group doesn't fancy it!

It's also worth bearing in mind that on two occasions I couldn't complete first attempts of these walks. One of these was in the Cairngorms when the wind speed was later recorded at 81mph, and another time was on Snowdon when the top of the Pyg Track was iced up and I didn't have an ice axe or crampons.

With all these warnings said, all the routes should be within the capabilities of an experienced hillwalker with good navigational skills.

The pubs

Combining a great walk with a great pub or two at the end of it was surprisingly tricky. Often the best mountains are in remote areas where the best pubs are not. Where possible, I've chosen walks that end right in a village or at a pub, but occasionally that couldn't happen; for example in Snowdonia or the sparsely populated Highlands. The pubs in these routes are nearby, however.

In choosing the pubs, I relied upon CAMRA's local expertise and asked for advice from the local branches for suggestions. As a result, the vast majority of the pubs in this book are also mentioned in my constant companion, the *Good Beer Guide*. Where they are not, they were perhaps chosen for their enduring links with mountain and climbing culture or were simply great pubs serving great beer. In particular, I like a pub with a 'muddy boots welcome' sign, a fantastic beer garden or a log fire, where I could easily drop in for a post-walk pint and be made to feel welcome.

I hope that you enjoy all of these walks and pubs as much as I have enjoyed sharing them with you.

Daniel Neilson, May 2017

The Bear, Crickhowell, Wales

How to use this book

The walks in this book have been carefully designed to give you all the information you will need to safely enjoy your days out in some of Britain's wild landscapes – and to find your way to the best pubs afterwards. Here is an overview of how to use the book:

▲ **Walk locator map**

This can be found on page 6. It shows the locations of the 22 walks, which are spread across England, Scotland and Wales.

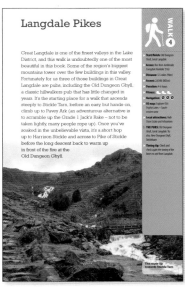

▲ **Walk information**

Located on the first page of each walk, a walk information panel provides the key practical details you will need to plan your day. They include the start and end points; how to access the walk; the walk distance, ascent and duration; an indication of the required fitness level and navigational difficulty – both from 1 to 4; the OS sheet map that covers the area of the route; a note on any local attractions; the names of the pubs visted; and timing tips. Further information about the walk, such as about the terrain covered, can often be found in the opening paragraph.

KEY TO SYMBOLS USED IN THIS BOOK	
🚶	Walk start
--➔--	Walk route
··●··	Alternative route
2	Pub location
Ⓐ	Waypoint
🧭 AB123123	OS grid reference
🛏	Accommodation available

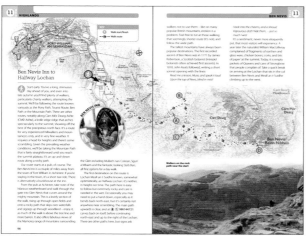

◀ **Ordnance Survey mapping**

The routes are plotted using either 1:25,000- or 1:50,000-scale Ordnance Survey mapping with suggested detours clearly marked. The start 🚶, waypoints Ⓐ with 6-figure grid references, and featured pubs 🍺 are marked on the map as shown.

▲ **Walk descriptions**

Detailed walk descriptions are designed to be followed in conjunction with the maps. Waypoints with OS grid references are provided at key points along each route. Featured pubs are numbered as they are visited along the route with 'Try also' pubs (green icons) numbered after the main entries.

▲ **Feature boxes**

Throughout the book, special feature boxes give detailed insights into fascinating local places, landscapes, people and history.

▲ **Pub information**

A box at the end of each walk provides information about featured pubs, including their address, opening hours, contact details, and whether accommodation is offered. As opening hours are subject to change – especially in rural areas – if you are relying on a pub being open, it is recommended that you phone ahead to check. Where accommodation is offered, it can range from camping barns to luxury bed and breakfast rooms. No assessment is made of quality or price.

Safety first

The mountains and coastal paths of Britain are often underestimated; both in terms of their beauty – watch as a new visitor to the Highlands stares agog at the scale of the mountains – but also in terms of their danger. The weather in the mountains is harsh and can often take unexpected turns, even in summer – snow on the uplands is not unheard of in July. Even if the weather seems benign in the valleys, on the tops it can be very harsh. When researching this book, on two occasions I had to turn back, and that was just fine. Mountain rescuers have told me that often the serious problems occur when a visitor to the area is so determined to do their planned walk, especially if they have come a long way for a short amount of time, that they carry on towards the summit despite all the warnings. If it seems dangerous, it probably is. Listen to yourself. But also listen to other members of your group, even if they are inexperienced. Blithely following a perceived leader is another common trap that can lead to accidents.

That said, with the right precautions, gear, planning and skills, a day on the mountains, even in poor weather, will be a rewarding experience at worst; and at best? Well, there's nothing on earth like it.

A climber in the Cairngorms

Remember too, that this is a summer walking guidebook and should not be used as a guide in winter or when there is snow and ice on the ground.

Planning

"In the mountains," I was once told. "It's not only important to have a plan 'B', but also a plan 'C', 'D' and 'E'." It's something I've always remembered. What that means is that while your route maybe drawn on OS maps reproduced in guidebooks such as this one, it's important to truly understand the route – where are the danger spots? Where are the escape routes? Are there places where a member of your party will feel uncomfortable? Is it beyond the physical capability of a member of your group? Has there been a lot of rain recently – what if a steam is impassable or a part of the route too slippery?

It is always imperative to carry a full OS map alongside those reproduced in books, ideally at 1:25,000 scale. If you do need to take a detour, or change the route, you need to be able to see the bigger context, which may not be shown on the map in the guidebook.

I also obsess over the weather, checking the Mountain Weather Information Service (**mwis.org.uk**) for the preceding days, and on the morning of the walk. This fantastic service covers the upland areas of Britain and covers all the regions that have walks in this book. The Met Office (**metoffice.gov.uk**) also publish a mountain weather service.

Nothing beats local knowledge however, and a pub near the walk is a great source for this information – most in this book get a lot of walkers in! Where possible, I'll always ask about the trail, about bridges and about streams that need to be crossed. This type of information can sometimes be gleaned from the National Parks' websites too. I'll always look at this the day before.

Public transport can also be tricky in these remote areas and buses will often

Approaching the attractive harbour at Staithes, North Yorkshire

run a different timetable on weekends and school holidays. I've suggested where there are buses, but don't rely on these alone as timetables can often change or switch. A good source for national bus information is Traveline (**traveline.info / 0871 200 22 33**).

Occasionally, you'll need to walk along the roads – common sense prevails.

Skills

This book assumes a certain level of skill and understanding of mountain and upland walking. The key skill, of course, is navigation. Knowing how to use a map and compass is an essential component for this book – the route descriptions themselves rely on an understanding of grid references and compass directions. Remember, too, that a compass doesn't tell you where you are, but where you are going. Nor does a map tell you where you are unless you are following it. I always have the map in my hand and my thumb on my location, and from reading the map I'll be looking out for what I expect to see next, such as steep ground, a path crossroads, a small lake.

A big debate continues around digital navigation. My thoughts on it are quite simple: is it a great extra tool to have? Yes. Can it be relied on solely? Absolutely not. Digital navigation does tell you where you are – and for that it's great. I have used a GPS and will always have a fully charged smartphone with me with mapping and location apps (for example, ViewRanger, OS Maps, and apps that give you your grid reference without the need for data such as OS Locate and GridPoint GB). Rarely, however, does the battery life survive for the whole day on a smartphone when using the apps, especially in the cold where it could last a matter of hours. As well as the fact that technologies can fail, they also suffer from the same issue as a guidebook, in that it is difficult to get a bigger picture of the terrain if your plans do have to change.

If you don't have these skills yet, don't worry, you have a great weekend ahead of you if you book yourself on a course at Plas y Brenin in Snowdonia or Glenmore Lodge in the Cairngorms, two fantastic outdoor training centres that offer a multitude of courses (I've done several). The courses will give you the foundation and open up a whole new, wonderful world of walking in Britain's mountains. The courses are informative, very affordable and brilliant fun.

Clothing & equipment

The right clothing is essential for days out on the mountain, and as you get more experienced you'll understand exactly what you need. For clothing, work on a layering system from the inside out. Without getting into the painstaking detail that I could do, for your top half, I'd recommend a base layer (synthetic or wool, not cotton), a mid layer such as a fleece or sweater and a waterproof jacket. I also usually take a synthetic (rather than down) insulated layer for those sandwich breaks. I also generally take a second, lightweight mid layer.

Gloves and a hat are essential, no matter what the weather when you set off. I take a minimum of two pairs of gloves, and nearly always three when it's cold: a soft pair of liner gloves, mitts or heavyweight gloves and a spare pair. A woolly hat is better than a synthetic one to regulate your temperature.

For your bottom half, a pair of synthetic walking trousers and waterproof overtrousers will usually suffice for summer walking. I wear very comfortable merino socks – it's important to get good socks as cheap ones can be a cause of blisters. I'm not a fan of gaiters but many people swear by them.

As for footwear, then nothing beats a pair of good walking boots, particularly leather ones. That said, in summer on lower-level walks I'll often wear training shoes. On most of the mountain walks in this book I'd wear boots. Most important here is fit and your local outdoor shop is the best place to advise.

In your backpack, you'll need food (including some sugary snacks to share!); plenty of water (I usually take a litre in a bottle with a filter on it from the likes of LifeStraw or Water-to-Go); a first aid kit designed for the outdoors (along with any personal medication etc.); a whistle; plasters or Compeed patches for blisters; a head torch and spare batteries and bulb; sunglasses; sun cream; a spare mid layer, socks and gloves; and a multitool. My map will be in my hand and my compass attached to the pocket of my jacket or around my wrist. I nearly always take an emergency group shelter too – they are lightweight and cheap.

With all of these things organised you should be ready to set off!

GLOSSARY OF MOUNTAIN AND HILLWALKING TERMS

Arête – a narrow mountain ridge separating two valleys.

Bealach – a pass, usually a low point between two hills (Scotland).

Bothy – an old shelter or shepherd's hut that is maintained as a shelter for hillwalkers.

Buttress – a prominent feature extending from the side of a hill or mountain.

Cairn – a human-made pile of stones, or sometimes a stone shelter, marking a trail.

Cirque or **corrie** (Scotland); **cwm** (Wales) – a bowl-shaped glaciated mountain valley, open on its downhill side and often with a small lake at the bottom.

Clough – see Gully.

Col – the lowest point along a ridge between two mountains, often being a pass.

Corrie loch – see Tarn.

Crag or **creag** (Scotland); **craig** (Wales) – a steep rocky outcrop or cliff.

Gully, **gill** or **ghyll** – a ravine or narrow, steep-sided valley created by the action of water.

Scramble – a slope that is steep enough to require the use of hands, but not a rock climb. Scrambles are graded with 1 being the easiest and 3 the hardest. A rope is advised certainly from Grade 2 and up, sometimes for Grade 1 scrambles if exposed.

Scree – loose rocks on a steep incline.

Tarn – a mountain lake or pool formed in a cirque.

England

Kinder Scout from Hayfield

WALK
1

Kinder Scout is always an adventure. This great moorland plateau, seared off at the top like a Belgian barman wipes the effervescent head off a beer, provides one of the best days out in Britain. The sense of adventure comes from the remoteness and the glorious panoramas of northern England. This walk starts out at Hayfield, a picturesque village blessed with several great pubs. We then follow the route of the Kinder Trespass of 1932, an event in history that opened up the English countryside for the world to enjoy, before joining part of the Pennine Way, which, without this action, may not have existed. So, after this one, you might want to raise a pint to Benny Rothman and his band of ramblers who changed access to the mountains forever.

▶ **Start/Finish:** Hayfield

▶ **Access:** Train from Manchester or Sheffield to New Mills, then bus from New Mills. Buses also from Glossop, Buxton & Stockport

▶ **Distance:** 10.5 miles (16km)

▶ **Ascent:** 2421ft (738m)

▶ **Duration:** 4-6 hours

▶ **Fitness:**

▶ **Navigation:** ✪ ✪ ✪

▶ **OS map:** Explorer OL1 *Peak District – Dark Peak area*

▶ **Local attractions:** Kinder Scout, Kinder Trespass heritage

▷ **THE PUBS:** Dutsons, George Hotel, Royal Hotel, all Hayfield; Lantern Pike, Little Hayfield

▶ **Timing tip:** Beware of streams after heavy rainfall.

Along the western edge of Kinder Scout

The village of Hayfield is a delightful place, interwoven with waterways and steep, narrow paths. It has long been an important staging post – since Roman times it has slaked the thirst of travellers between Buxton and Glossop. Wool and paper became two of the most important industries in the village at the time of the Industrial Revolution. When the trains arrived (they've since disappeared), they began to not only take goods to Manchester, but also to bring people in to explore the countryside, including early ramblers. Today, it's hillwalkers, fell runners and mountain bikers who make Hayfield a fantastic base for exploring Kinder Scout. Notably the Pennine Bridleway passes through the village. It's also home to the rather busy Kinder Mountain Rescue Team (whose services we hope not to need as we're taking a fairly straightforward route).

We start at the main bus stop and Hayfield Countryside Centre for our long day out. Cross the busy road and head towards the church past Dutsons, a restaurant and cafe with a good line in local beers. At St Matthew's Church turn right on to Church Street, then bear left on to Valley Road where you'll see green signs with an acorn and the letters 'PBW'. This is the Pennine Bridleway which our route briefly skips along.

This pleasant stretch of path runs along the River Kinder, which tumbles down from Kinder Reservoir, and the first destination of our day. At a fork in the path at **A** SK044866, we leave the Pennine Bridleway, go through some old gates, and then continue along the river past a campsite. A fingerpost reads: 'Bowden Bridge Car Park and Kinder Scout'. At the entrance to the campsite there's a road bridge that leads directly to the Bowden Bridge car park. High in the rocks by

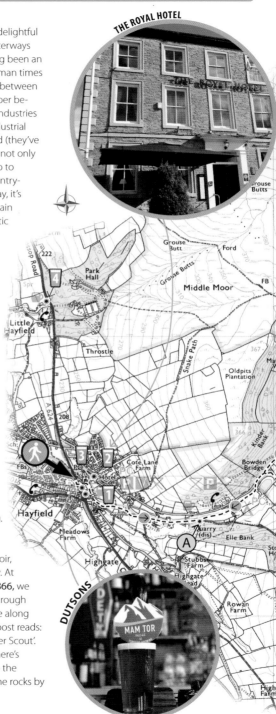

THE ROYAL HOTEL

DUTSONS

KEY

🚶 Walk start/finish

┅┅► Walk route

ygatehead Moor

624

Ford

Fords

Fords

Fords

Fords

Fords

Ford

Fords

Ford

William Clough

Sandy Heys

Fords

Kinder Downfall

Ford

FB

Nab Brow

Hollin Head

White Brow

Fords

FB

Ford

Kinder Reservoir

Blackshaws

Kinder Head

Upper Moor

Upper House

Kinder Reservoir

Pennine Way

Ford

HAYFIELD CP

ds

Ford

Kinder Scout National Nature Reserve

Broad Clough

B

Sheep Wash

The Three Knolls

Fords

Kinder Low

633

Cairn

Noe Stool

Ford

Tunstead Clough Farm

Sheepfold

Cairn

Edale Rocks

nstead ouse

Kinderlow Cavern

603

The Ashes

Kinderlow End

Fords

Ford

Swine's Back

C

Stony Ford

Sheepfold

533

Sheepfold

Harry Moor

Ford

Ford

Edale Cross

541

Oaken Clough

Valve Chamber

Sheepfold

Rain Gauge

D

HIGH PEAK DISTRICT

559

Coldwell Clough

Ford

FB

South Head Farm

Shelter

Sheepfold

Rain Gauge

Looking across Kinder Reservoir

the entrance to the car park is a plaque that reads: 'The mass trespass onto Kinder Scout started from this quarry 24th April 1932'. It was unveiled in 1982 by Benny Rothman, one of the key figures in the trespass, then aged 70. Our route follows the one those brave souls took up to Kinder Scout. Duly inspired, start in their footsteps and follow Kinder Road north. A fingerpost points you in the direction of 'Kinder Scout via William Clough or Farlands'.

At the entrance to Kinder Reservoir is Booth sheepwash and a small information placard relating the history of sheep washing here. With around 500 sheep it is something that would last for days and was turned into a social occasion.

Cross the stone bridge and walk along the lane briefly. Straight ahead you'll see the footpath that runs alongside the river. The path then crosses the river again and you'll rejoin the lane to the reservoir. Beside the main gate to the reservoir, you'll see a pedestrian gate with a sign informing you that you'll be entering the National Trust's White Brow. A dauntingly steep cobbled path leads up. Climb this path until it levels out, opening up stunning views across the reservoir towards Kinder Downfall, a destination later in the day.

The true size of Kinder Scout can now also be seen. It's a vast hulking mass of Millstone Grit covered in heather and peat. Its highest point is 636m (and you'll hit 633m).

Continue along the path preparing yourself for a switchback – you don't see the sign (marked 'Bridleway') until you're almost upon it. Resist the temptation to climb back earlier along little paths. Just past the turning is an information board about the reservoir that, after a lengthy and troubled construction, opened in 1912 to serve water to the people of Stockport. The bridleway

The seemingly flat Kinder Plateau is anything but

rises west to meet another signposted track. I have spent a lot of time walking around Kinder Scout, and I believe the views here to be among the best. The sign reads Snake Inn (unfortunately not our final destination) and the track continues to rise, and then fall, into William Clough. From here a soggy uphill slog brings you eventually onto the plateau.

Kinder Scout has a nomenclature all of its own: cloughs, groughs and grikes all feature – no wonder geologists get excited by it. We follow the clough as the water falls down it. There's plenty of stepping stone action as the path crosses the stream – be aware that after a lot of rainfall it could be tricky in places. It's a long, rocky path and boots are recommended here but there are still very few places where you need to put a hand down. The final push is along a rock staircase to a

A gritstone outcrop on Kinder Scout

very large cairn. Just after the cairn there is a stone footpath that leads to the steepest climb of the day, onto the plateau itself. It's also just before the climb where we meet the Pennine Way along part of its 267-mile (431-kilometre) journey from Edale to Kirk Yetholm on the Scottish Borders.

The mercifully short climb to another huge cairn welcomes you to Kinder Scout. Any walkers who have had the joy of crossing Kinder Scout in anything but fair weather will know of its navigational

challenges. Kinder is a moorland plateau, but it seems anything but flat once you are on it. There is a fairly clear path all around the plateau, above its gritstone edges and cloughs. Those readers who know Kinder and looked at the 'three boot' symbol for navigation and raised an eyebrow will now understand, as we are only skirting the edge, along the most used part of the trail. The main problem with navigation

Looking back over Kinder Reservoir

is the groughs, as the deep channels that cross the peak are deeper than a human is tall meaning you're running on your wits (well, map and compass). It's all too easy to follow the random swerving of a grough and become completely disorientated and lost, as people frequently do (on one occasion I met with Kinder Mountain Rescue on an exercise and during the day they had found two groups of people utterly lost on top). Louis J Jennings, writing in 1880 and collected in Roly Smith's *A Peak District Anthology*, describes Kinder Scout as 'one vast moor, intersected with long, broad gulches,

and abounding in deep holes, patches of wet moss, and pools of dark water … The scenery is an ample recompense for all the trouble – a more glorious mountain view there cannot be in England.' If you are crossing Kinder, then map, compass and keeping to the bearing are essential. Let's not even talk about winter. Kinder on a bleak day is a harsh place to be.

But no worries today, as the route we're following is fairly easy even in poor weather. As part of the Pennine Way, it's a well-worn route. There are occasional jumbles of rocks where the path seems imperceptible, but you'll find it again with ease.

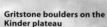

Gritstone boulders on the Kinder plateau

From the cairn, walk south-east along the edge to reach Kinder Downfall, the tallest waterfall in the Peak District at 30 metres. This is a popular place for climbers, particularly in winter when the falls can freeze making it good for a short dose of mountaineering and an opportunity to get your ice axe and crampons a bit scruffy. Don't expect more than a trickle in summer. In high winds, it's been known for the falls to appear as though they're going upwards.

We now start south, again along the edge, heading for the trig point at **B** ☻ SK078870. On a good day the peaks visible are astonishing: Snowdon some 94 miles away has been seen, as has Long Mynd at 71 miles distant. Manchester is easily seen.

The trig point is very nearly the highest point of Kinder and from here you'll get an amazing view of the Vale of Edale, and across the southern edge of Kinder Scout, including the distinctive Woolpacks stone formation.

The path is somewhat indistinct here, more a jumble of stones. In poor weather, definitely take a compass bearing. Hopefully, you'll be able to see Edale Rocks, a large mass of rocks (and a brilliant place to shelter from the wind – have your sandwich here, not at the trig point). The path goes to the left of Edale Rocks and soon becomes clearly paved. Continue downhill, but at **C** ☻ SK080861, keep straight to the wooden fence below. (The footpath left, and the route of the Pennine Way, heads down Jacob's Ladder towards Edale.)

At the gate, turn right on to the bridleway that heads directly west. This bridleway is popular with mountain bikers either trudging up or throwing themselves down. It's a rough road, and not particularly easy

THE KINDER TRESPASS

It's hard to imagine, that in 1932 there was no access land in England and no public footpaths. Despite this the rambling movement had been burgeoning since the Industrial Revolution when workers would leave the smog-ridden towns and cities to seek some fresh air in the countryside.

The Kinder Mass Trespass was organised by the Manchester branch of the British Workers Sports Federation after their members were turned away by gamekeepers on nearby Bleaklow some weeks earlier. On that April morning, more than 400 people – the majority setting out from Bowden Bridge and some setting out from Edale, assembled to walk and protest against the lack of access to the countryside. They walked up William Clough, where this route heads. But they met gamekeepers towards the top where there were scuffles, although no one was seriously hurt. They went on to meet the other group of ramblers, but on their return to Hayfield five members of the party, including Benny Rothman, were arrested and kept in Hayfield Lock-Up. They were subsequently charged with unlawful assembly and breach of the peace. Five of the six were found guilty and jailed for between two and six months. It caused a huge amount of media attention around the world, most of it sympathetic with the trespassers. It united the cause and several weeks later, more than 10,000 ramblers held a rally at Winnats Pass near Castleton. It is argued that it led directly to the National Parks legislation in 1949, and the National Trail network.

The first National Trail was the Pennine Way that this route joins for a while. However, the vision set out by Rothman and his cohorts only really came to fruition with the Countryside and Rights of Way Act 2000 (known as CROW) that legislated on rights to walk on mapped access land. The fight for further rights continues in England and Wales who look to the more progressive land use in Scotland, and there are similar problems with access to waterways. But what happened on that day in 1932 set forward the movement that today allows us access to our wild places.

George Hotel

Dutsons

walking. At **D** SK077860 be sure to take note of Edale Cross, a stone cross thought to be medieval, that marks the three wards of Glossop, Longdendale and Hopedale.

It's down and down now until you see the paved road that you're longing for after this stony descent. Then follow the lane back to Bowden Bridge car park.

From here, take the route you came up on, past the campsite and along the river back into Hayfield itself.

As mentioned earlier, there are several good pub options in Hayfield and two of them, the **George Hotel** and the **Royal Hotel**, are *Good Beer Guide*

regulars. The first one you'll come to is the George Hotel. Despite the somewhat worn sign, it's a pleasant pub with a roaring cast-iron range when it's chilly. It's been around since the 16th century and was originally built as a mail house. The Derby Militia was formed here in 1808. The stained glass windows are noteworthy as is the beer range. There were four pumps on when I visited with Banks's Bitter supported by a couple from local breweries.

The Royal Hotel, just past St Matthew's Church and over the bridge, is a grand Georgian coaching inn with roaring fires, oak panels and books on the shelves. It's a popular venue for Sunday lunch. For me, though, the draw is the wooden-floored Ramblers bar littered with retired walking boots and some interesting early climbing memorabilia. There are some lovely photos of the local area, some contemporary, some showing early enthusiasts in full tweed suits. It's the kind of place that lists the Hayfield Fell Races. On the bar is a good selection of real ales, including Kinder Falldown that is brewed for the hotel by Lancashire's Happy Valley Brewery.

Finally, between the Royal Hotel and the bus stop, is **Dutsons**, somewhere between a deli and a restaurant. Either way, it's a good place to grab a quick pint of locally produced beer or a couple of bottles to leave with.

Also worth a look is the **Lantern Pike** about 10 minutes further along the road towards Glossop. It's another *Good Beer Guide* regular and is particularly good for food.

PUB INFORMATION

1 **GEORGE HOTEL**
14 Church Street, Hayfield SK22 2JE
01663 743691 • georgehotelhayfield.co.uk •
Opening hours: 11.45-11 (11.30 Fri & Sat); 12-11 Sun

2 **ROYAL HOTEL**
Market Street, Hayfield, SK22 2EP
01663 742721 • theroyalathayfield.com •
Opening hours: 11-11

3 **DUTSONS**
Steeple End Fold, Hayfield, SK22 2JD
01663 741404 • dutsons.co.uk
Opening hours: 11-7 (11 Wed & Thu; midnight Fri & Sat; 10.30 Sun)

4 **LANTERN PIKE**
45 Glossop Road, Little Hayfield, SK22 2NG
01663 747590 • lanternpikeinn.co.uk •
Opening hours: 12-3 (not Mon); 5-11; 12-11 Sat & Sun

Bamford circular

The Vale of Edale sweeps down from the mighty Kinder Scout in the north and up to the ridge between Lose Hill and Mam Tor in the south. In between, the seemingly year-round verdancy of the vale is a proud sight. This walk, conveniently on a regular train line, starts out from Bamford to summit Win Hill before dipping down and back up again to Lose Hill, then crosses a ridge towards Mam Tor. Before reaching the 'Shivering Mountain' it descends into Hope and to the first pub, the quaint old Cheshire Cheese. The final cross-country walk brings you back to Bamford and the community-owned Anglers Rest. It's a walk that offers 360-degree views over the best of the Peak District before seeking out some of its finest pubs, and even a little brewery.

▷ **Start/finish:** Bamford

▷ **Access:** Train between Manchester and Sheffield

▷ **Distance:** 13 miles (21km)

▷ **Ascent:** 2559ft (780m)

▷ **Duration:** 6-7 hours

▷ **Fitness:**

▷ **Navigation:**

▷ **OS map:** Explorer OL1 *Peak District – Dark Peak area*

▷ **Local attractions:** Stunning views across the Peak District from Win and Lose hills

▷ **THE PUBS:** YHA Castleton Losehill Hall, Hope Valley; Cheshire Cheese, Hope; Anglers Rest, Bamford. Try also: Woodroffe Arms, Old Hall Hotel, both Hope

From Bamford rail station, walk up to the bridge, onto Station Road and head north towards Bamford village. It's a short walk along the pavement before taking the first left past a car mechanics onto Water Lane, across a bridge, then on past some playing fields to a couple of large buildings. On the other side of the buildings, there's a narrow and leafy footpath on the right that leads north to the hamlet of Thornhill. As the path comes out onto the road in Thornhill, turn right and then left at the fork straight ahead of you. There's no pavement here so beware of cars, but you're more likely to see cyclists. At Townhead Lane turn right up the road until it turns into a path and follow the signs to Win Hill.

As the path opens out over a wall, start to walk uphill around to the east of the knoll. Views back to Bamford and over Ladybower

Reservoir will appear. The Derwent Dam, that separates the Ladybower and Derwent reservoirs, was used for target practice by Lancaster bombers six weeks before the famous Dambusters raid in World War II.

At the junction, turn right onto the grassy path and past a sign that points back to Thornhill. It's likely to be only skittish sheep you encounter along this path. At the fork **A** 🔗 SK192845 stay to the left and follow a fingerpost that points towards a plantation to the right of a handsome stone wall.

Once among the trees, another fingerpost points uphill towards Win Hill through a pleasant, rocky glade. The scattered path follows a route through the trees before emerging on a clear stone path rising steeply towards the summit. Here the views really open out to the south over the Peak District National Park and beyond its borders. It's a

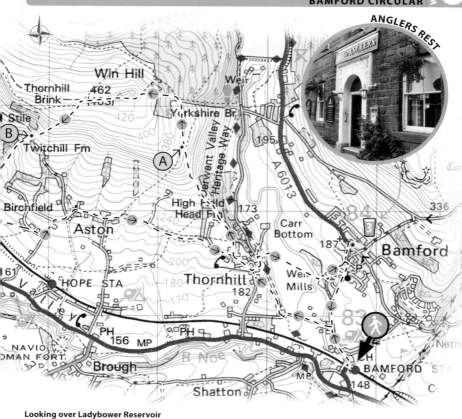

Looking over Ladybower Reservoir

WARD AND THE SHEFFIELD CLARION RAMBLERS

Bert Ward, a Labour Party politician and founder member of the Youth Hostels Association (YHA), set up the Sheffield Clarion Ramblers Club in 1900. The group was named after the socialist *Clarion* newspaper and affiliated with the Labour Representation Committee, a forerunner of the Labour Party. The Clarion Rambling Club was largely a campaigning group looking for access to moorland in the Peak District. In recognition of his role in the campaigning work of the group, the Sheffield and District Federation of the Ramblers Association gifted part of Lose Hill to Bert Ward in 1945. He then subsequently gave it to the National Trust. The Ordnance Survey still calls this area 'Lose Hill or Ward's Piece'.

peaceful and green view. At the top of Win Hill is Win Hill Pike, a knobbly outcrop known locally as the 'pimple'. Once the summit trig point is reached a huge vista opens out to the more melancholy northern moors.

There's a story about how Win Hill and Lose Hill, the next destination of the day,

Walkers on the top of Win Hill

got their names. It relates to a battle that was supposedly fought on the hills between warring princes after the withdrawal of the Roman army opened up a power vacuum. It is, sadly, a fanciful construction since it has been discovered that the hill was originally called Wythinehull, meaning Willow Hill.

From the trig point you can almost see the route of the whole walk. The spiky Lose Hill is clear, and dauntingly far away. You can also follow the ridge all the way along to Mam Tor, safe in the knowledge that we're only doing about two-thirds of the ridge before descending back to civilisation.

From the summit, start descending to the west of the satisfying protuberance, and follow the path downhill. Here you'll see the path continue around and then to the north, leading along the ridge. (For a longer walk, you could head down the ridge before skirting up the southern side of Kinder Scout, and then descend into Edale and to the doors of the Ram's Head Inn.)

This walk, however, only goes a short way along the ridge, turning off left at the first stile and down, and down, along a rocky

path. At the kissing gate, **B** ⊙ SK179847, the route is a little unclear, but just head directly down south-west to the gate in the wall, with the cottages just visible down below to the right. Once at the wall, you'll be able to see the cottages clearly. Walk down this steep hill to the gate by the first cottage. Walk through the yard, where there are several holiday homes, and down the paved road. The road weaves around to the right and under the railway. Follow Bowden Lane back round to the left, past a green footpath sign and some cottages, and across the superbly named Killhill Bridge that arcs over the River Noe. At the end of the lane is Edale Road and down to the right is the Cheshire Cheese. Resist the temptation to call it a day here (there's still the majority of the walk to go) and cross the road to the public footpath opposite. Head through a stone stile, past a house on the left and a farm on the right.

Then turn at the first footpath on the right and follow the path to cross through many gates and fields. You'll also cross a bridge over the train line with the faintly alarming sign that warns: 'Only 20 persons allowed on this bridge at any one time'. The bridge genuinely wobbles as you cross!

At the other side follow the footpath signs through a gate and then what seems like someone's backyard before emerging into fields again. On one of the fence posts is a small plaque commemorating Frederick H Fox 'a Member of the Sheffield Clarion Ramblers Club 1912-1962'. He would have certainly known about the Kinder Trespass (see Walk 1) that eventually led to rights to use the footpaths across England's wild country.

Follow a large green sign that reads 'Public Footpath to Mam Tor via Losehill Farm'. From Losehill Farm it's a short trot up to the

summit of Lose Hill, crossing a large stile over a wire fence for the final climb.

From the top of Lose Hill there are amazing views over the Vale of Edale and towards Kinder Scout above – it looking every bit the flattened plateau it is. To the west is the Great Ridge that we'll be following, with Mam Tor rising high two miles further. Also visible is the summit of Win Hill; this is probably the best perspective of it.

Walk along the undulating ridge as far as Hollins Cross at **C** 📍 **SSK136845.** If you're feeling sprightly then it's just over a kilometre from here to the summit of Mam Tor. The route over Hollins Cross is an ancient path used by people crossing from Edale to Castleton. Before a church was built in Edale in 1663, parishioners would carry their dead over this route to bury them in the churchyard in Castleton. Later, in the 18th and 19th centuries, women and children from Castleton would traverse Hollins Cross to work in a cotton mill in Edale.

From the cross, descend steeply to the south-east across open fields and down a rocky path until you hit a small lane marked Hollowford Road. Follow this towards

The northern end of Ladybower Reservoir from Win Hill

Castleton, and take the second left down Robinlands Lane – a small fingerpost points to a public footpath down this way. You will pass a playground and playing field, heading towards the Rotary Centre Castleton. As the road bends sharply at a right angle to the left, follow the footpath across the field to emerge onto another non-paved lane. At **D** 📍 SK153838 is the rear entrance to 🏠 **YHA Castleton Losehill Hall**, a large and lovely youth hostel particularly notable for being home to Hope Valley Brewing Company. There's a gap in the stone wall to access the car park and you can walk straight through the hostel's front door. It's always worth a look around the bar to see what's on tap.

Continue east along the path to Spring House Farm. Turn left through the farmyard and past the horse stables where the route continues east down a boggy path over a stile. At **E** 📍 SK164842 you'll hit a lane that you've already walked up towards Lose Hill. Follow this back over the wobbly bridge then follow the same path to emerge onto Edale Road. Turn left and walk north along Edale Road. Be careful of the cars as it's fairly busy and there's no pavement. After a short

Lose Hill

distance you'll arrive at the **2 Cheshire Cheese**, a delightful old pub across three rooms, all on different levels. The building now housing the inn was built in 1632 as two cottages – look out for one of the original doorways next to the pub entrance. The cottages sat on the route for sheep drovers and before then salt merchants. Today, it's a popular pub with walkers and on my visit there were beers from Thornbridge, Acorn, Abbeydale and Peak Ales. Two handpumps offer an ever-changing range of ales. It's the kind of pub with a collection box for the local mountain rescue team and therefore the kind of pub I like.

Now, there is an option here to head into Hope where there are a couple of other reasonable pub options, including the **4 Woodroffe Arms**, and the **5 Old Hall Hotel**. Also here is a train station on the cross Pennine route – where you can catch a train to the next station of Bamford – just saying!

The final stretch of the walk from here to Bamford takes around an hour. To continue, walk back down Edale Road and turn left to Killhill Bridge. Once over the bridge, turn immediately right onto a leafy lane that winds along the River Noe. Follow the footpath through the mill, until you reach an open field. Here look out for the tunnel under the railway line that splits off at a right angle to the river. Once out of the tunnel, cut diagonally across the field along a slightly worn path to the right of the campsite. Turn right onto the lane and then left on Aston Lane to rise up towards the hamlet of Aston. Again, it's a quiet road but be aware of cars. As the road curves steeply to the left, there's a fingerpost and a wide footpath that leads directly east behind the houses. Walk down here and descend towards the road again. From here it's a lengthy walk back into Thornhill along the lane - be wary of traffic, especially around the tight corners. There are, however, plenty of passing places.

Anglers Rest

In Thornhill, follow the road that leads around to the left called Carr Lane (to the right you'll recognise the beginning of the walk). As another private road splits off the main road, there's a fingerpost marked Bamford Mill, the next destination. Descend steeply through the field – there were cows in it on my trip – and through another gate.

PUB INFORMATION

1 YHA CASTLETON LOSEHILL HALL
Hope Valley, S33 8WB • 0345 371 9628
yha.org.uk • 🛏
Opening hours: 12-10.30; 12-11 Sat & Sun

2 CHESHIRE CHEESE
Edale Road, Hope, S33 6ZF • 01433 620381
thecheshirecheeseinn.co.uk • 🛏
Opening hours: 12-3, 6-11; 12-11 Sat; 12-9 Sun;
closed Mon

3 ANGLERS REST
Main Road, Bamford, S33 0DY • 01433 659317
anglers.rest
Opening hours: 11-11 (midnight Sat); 12-11 Sun

Try also:

4 WOODROFFE ARMS
Castleton Road, Hope, S33 6SB • 01433 620351 • 🛏
Opening hours: 3-11 (midnight Fri); 1-midnight
Sat & Sun.

5 OLD HALL HOTEL
Market Place, Hope S33 6RH • 01433 620160
oldhallhotelhope.co.uk • 🛏
Opening hours: 8am-midnight

At the bottom, turn right following the footpath towards Bamford Mill. Here you'll come across a delightful wooden bridge that crosses the River Derwent above a weir. It's an exceedingly picturesque spot. In the middle of the bridge is an artwork on the Bamford Sculpture trail, indicative of the creative nature of this little village, seemingly home to dozens of artists.

Hop along the raised wooden platform to emerge at Bamford Mills, now converted into apartments, and turn left along the road, heading uphill to meet the main road. Turn left here and follow the road until you get to the **3 Anglers Rest**, a pub that has been owned by the community since 2013. When it was threatened with closure in 2012, the Bamford Community Society was founded to take the pub over. This required it to be recognised as a Community Asset, the first in Derbyshire. Then £263,000 was raised through selling community shares, enough to buy the pub. However, it was offered to a rival bid from a developer. After a long fight it opened in 2013 and a staff of 25 is now employed across the pub, village post office and a cafe. It's a heartening story. The Anglers offered local beers from Intrepid Brewery and Abbeydale on my visit. There's also an impressive food menu.

From here, give yourself a 20-minute hobble back down the road to the train station.

Coniston circular

The Old Man of Coniston, down in the southerly Furness fells, is often overlooked in favour of the more northerly mountains, but that would be to miss out on one of Lakeland's highlights. This straightforward but strenuous walk leaves from the village of Coniston and weaves its way through the fascinating industrial heritage that left its mark on the mountain, before emerging on the 803-metre peak, with surely some of the best views in England. The route then continues on high ground around Dow Crag before following the Walna Scar Road back into Coniston where three cosy pubs and a brewery await. There's also an option to shorten the walk a little.

▶ **Start/finish:** Black Bull Inn, Coniston

▶ **Access:** Regular buses from Ambleside to Coniston, and between Ambleside and Kendal/Oxenholme

▶ **Distance:** 7.5 miles (12km)

▶ **Ascent:** 2,860ft (872m)

▶ **Duration:** 4-6 hours

▶ **Fitness:**

▶ **Navigation:**

▶ **OS map:** Explorer OL6 *The English Lakes — South-western area*

▶ **Local attractions:** Brantwood, Ruskin Museum

▷ **THE PUBS:** Black Bull Inn, the Sun, Yewdale Inn, all in Coniston

▶ **Timing tip:** It's possible to shorten this walk by descending to Goat's Water from Goat's Hawse.

Looking over a cloud inversion from the top of the Old Man of Coniston

Coniston to the Old Man of Coniston summit

Coniston is a lovely little village with a history full of interest and intrigue. It first attracted farmers and miners who found their living from digging out copper and slate. Later,

Old mining equipment on the Old Man of Coniston

Coniston Water became a comfort and a muse to the poet, art critic and social visionary John Ruskin (see box on page 36). Other writers and artists found inspiration in the village including Ruskin's contemporary Arthur Ransome who based his *Swallows and Amazons* series on Coniston. But it was probably the world water speed record attempt on Coniston Water by Donald Campbell (see page 39) that attracted most attention for the village. The final daring attempt sadly ended in tragedy.

Our walk starts in the centre of the village by the Black Bull Inn, an old coaching inn dating back 400 years and home to the Coniston Brewing Company. From behind the pub, cross the bridge that spans Church Beck, turn immediately right and walk up to the Sun. A post on the road leading right around the pub is marked with two signs pointing to Old Man

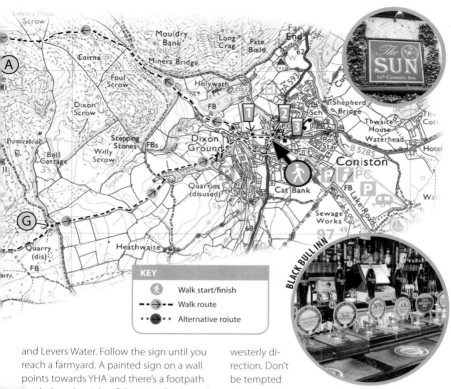

KEY

🚶 Walk start/finish

•–•→•–• Walk route

•••➤••• Alternative roiute

BLACK BULL INN

and Levers Water. Follow the sign until you reach a farmyard. A painted sign on a wall points towards YHA and there's a footpath symbol on the right of the gate. Go through the yard, following the footpath north-west. This pleasant part of the walk follows Church Beck, before arching in a more westerly direction. Don't be tempted to cross the beck towards YHA Coniston Coppermines, but continue on the path west gaining height all the time.

**Looking north from the
Old Man of Coniston**

Looking back up toward Buck Pike

As you climb you'll start to see the scars of the area's industrial heritage. The Coppermines valley was heavily mined for copper and slate, as well as nickel and cobalt. There are two slate mines still operating in the area: one to the north of you and the other just south of our walk up to the summit. The copper mines of Coniston date back to Elizabethan times, but it wasn't until the 19th century that technology enabled

JOHN RUSKIN

London-born John Ruskin had been attracted to the Lake District since his father took him there on a 'tour' as a young boy. It must have made an indelible mark. Ruskin was born in 1819 to a well-to-do family with great connections across Europe. He is best described as a polymath. A critic and patron, he had a great passion for art (especially the work of Turner) and became Slade Professor of Art at Oxford. But he also had a deep and yearning sense of social justice. His wealth allowed him to become an educational philanthropist, who sought to implement change in society. He was an early advocate for the welfare state, minimum wage, a national health service and environmental protection. Ruskin bought Brantwood, a large house on the shores of Coniston Water, unseen in

1871, seeking a country escape, and he spent the last 28 years of his life there writing and painting. Among regular visitors at Brantwood were artists Arthur Severn and William Gershom Collingwood as well as Arthur Ransome, who learned to sail in Collingwood's boat, Swallow – the inspiration for the *Swallows and Amazons* books. Brantwood (brantwood.org.

Brantwood

people to fully mine the depths of the area. Copper mining stopped in 1914. The mine manager's building that you can see in the valley became a hostel in 1931, the first of the Youth Hostel Association's network in the Lake District. It's a great place to stay.

Slate mines have been around for even longer than the copper mines, certainly they were up and running by the 1500s. Yet the valley has been settled since at least Bronze Age times – some of the cairns we pass probably date back to this period.

There's a clear path for most of the way up to the summit and there's a surprising number of industrial remains on the eastern slopes of the mountain. It's actually a little spooky when the mist is down. These were once some of the largest mines in England and now the shelters and mechanical beasts that transported the heavy rock down from these slopes remain in a dilapidated state. The amount of industrial remains means it's important not to leave the path: there are shafts and steep cuts all around.

At **A** 🌀 SD284981 there's a crossroads in the path, but continue straight on, rising up the increasingly steep path, through the disused quarries. While the path is clear it is important to not get too distracted by the

machinery as short paths do lead off in all directions. Once you reach Low Water at **B** 🌀 SD275982 the path gets even steeper as it heads up the east ridge of the mountain. Steep ground surrounds three sides of the Old Man of Coniston, giving it a thrilling aspect as it rises high above Coniston Water, and you a vertiginous feeling as you ascend.

Follow this rough path higher and higher until it begins to flatten out a little. Before you know it you'll be at the summit cairn atop a platform made of slate, of course. On a clear day the prospect is one of the best in England, with views as far as the Blackpool Tower, Morecambe Bay and the Isle of Man. Along the ridge to the north is Swirl How and immediately to the west is Dow Crag, the next destination of the walk.

Old Man of Coniston summit to Walna Scar Road

From the summit of the Old Man of Coniston at **C** 🌀 SD272978, follow the clear path roughly north-west (avoiding the huge drop to the north), but look

Blind Tarn from Buck Pike

Looking back towards Buck Pike

out for the fork in the path at **D** SD271979 and take the left-hand path downhill, north and west. It's still fairly clear even in poor weather but I'd advise keeping an eye on your compass here. We're heading to the col at **E** SD265983, marked as Goat's Hawse on the OS map, above Goat's Water below you to the south.

The tarn is 15 metres deep and contains trout and char. You can make a decision here whether or not to head along the shorter route towards Walna Scar Road, saving just under a mile.

For the shorter walk – good if the weather is poor – descend the path that zigzags down to Goat's Water. It's steep but not too

Cloud covers the fells north of the Old Man

Walking along Walna Scar Road

treacherous. Follow the path that hugs the eastern side of the tarn, cuts below Goat Crag and then picks up Walna Scar Road at **F** 🕐 **SD273964.** The route continues in the next section (second paragraph).

To continue up to Dow Crag, simply follow the clear path from the col west and then south around the incredibly steep drop down towards Goat's Water. The cliffs below Dow Crag are well-known climbing crags. In clear weather the views from up here are spectacular, back towards Old Man and down to Coniston Water. The wonderful ridge rises up to Dow Crag at 778 metres, and then undulates south to Buck Pike at 744 metres. Again, beware of the steep drop to your left. Descend the clear path south to Brown Pike at 682 metres, where there's a cairn. The path then zigzags down to the west to meet the wide path that is the Walna Scar Road.

Walna Scar Road to Coniston

The Walna Scar Road is a pass (a restricted byway) that leads from Coniston to Duddon and Seathwaite. It's a wide path that has been used for hundreds of years and reaches a height of 608 metres. Once you've made it here it's now a long but pleasant trot back to Coniston. On a clear day there are great views down towards Coniston Water.

DONALD CAMPBELL

Like his father, Sir Malcolm Campbell, Donald Campbell was a daredevil. Malcolm Campbell had gained both the water and land speed records during the 1920s and 1930s in vehicles called Blue Bird. After his father's death in 1948, Donald resolved to set records again. Only a year or two after Malcolm's death, Donald was out on Coniston water in his father's old boat, now called Bluebird K4, reaching 170mph. This was soon outdone, but undeterred he continued his quest. Between 1955 and 1964 Donald Campbell set seven water speed records, on Ullswater and on Coniston, where Bluebird K7 appeared annually. In 1964 he reached speeds of 276mph. During the 1960s he focussed his attention on the land speed record, but to gain exposure for this, he attempted to push further his water speed record beyond 300mph. On January 4, 1967, he attempted the run again on Coniston and hit the measured kilometre marker at a peak speed of 318mph, but during this crucial kilometre Bluebird K7's nose lifted and it crashed, killing him. Campbell's body wasn't recovered until 2001. He was buried at St Andrew's Church in Coniston after his coffin was carried through the measured kilometre on the water. The Ruskin Museum (ruskinmuseum.com) has a display of Donald Campbell memorabilia. The current world water speed record is 318mph, set in 1978.

View of Long Crag from the Sun   **Drinkers outside the Black Bull**

If you've taken the shorter route you'll meet Walna Scar Road at **F** ⊙ SD273964. There are footpaths leading off the route but just stick to the widest one, staying left under the crags of the Old Man. At **G** ⊙ SD289970 there's a place for cars and the start of a sealed road back to Coniston. Hop onto the road here for the final kilometre back to the village. The lane makes a weaving descent and as the houses appear look out for a road on the left that leads to the **1 Sun** pub that you passed earlier. This *Good Beer Guide* regular is a fantastically cosy and friendly 16th-century inn with local slate flooring, exposed beams and up to eight cask ales served over the slate bar, many from local breweries. There's a great view from its beer garden too. The Sun was the base for Donald Campbell during his final water

speed record attempts and the Boat Room at the inn honours these associations.

From here, continue walking downhill to the **2 Black Bull** – you'll see it from over the river. The Black Bull is a large 16th-century coaching inn that's popular with tourists, especially in summer. It is also notable for being the home of Coniston Brewing Company. As a result there's a wide range of beers on at any one time, including the multi award-winning Bluebird Bitter, named after the boat in which Donald Campbell attempted the water speed record.

The final pub is the popular **3 Yewdale Inn**, just across the road. There are stunning views from the outside terrace and a good choice of beers including the excellent Loweswater Gold from Cumbrian Legendary Ales. It's a friendly place to finish off a day's walking.

PUB INFORMATION

1 THE SUN
Sun Hill, Coniston, LA21 8HQ
015394 41248 • thesunconiston.com • 🍴
Opening hours: 11-11

2 BLACK BULL INN
Coniston, LA21 8DU
015394 41335 • blackbullconiston.co.uk • 🍴
Opening hours: 8.30-11

3 YEWDALE INN
Coniston, 2 Yewdale Road. LA21 8DU
015394 41280 • yewdaleinn.com • 🍴
Opening hours: 12-11

The Sun

Langdale Pikes

WALK 4

Great Langdale is one of the finest valleys in the Lake District, and this walk is undoubtedly one of the most beautiful in this book. Some of the region's biggest mountains tower over the few buildings in this valley. Fortunately for us three of those buildings in Great Langdale are pubs, including the Old Dungeon Ghyll, a classic hillwalkers pub that has little changed in years. It's the starting place for a walk that ascends steeply to Stickle Tarn, before an easy, but hands-on, climb up to Pavey Ark (an adventurous alternative is to scramble up the Grade 1 Jack's Rake – not to be taken lightly, many people rope up). Once you've soaked in the unbelievable vista, it's a short hop up to Harrison Stickle and across to Pike of Stickle before the long descent back to warm up in front of the fire at the Old Dungeon Ghyll.

▶ **Start/finish:** Old Dungeon Ghyll, Great Langdale

▶ **Access:** Bus from Ambleside (Langdale Rambler 516)

▶ **Distance:** 5.5 miles (9km)

▶ **Ascent:** 2,634ft (803m)

▶ **Duration:** 4-6 hours

▶ **Fitness:**

▶ **Navigation:**

▶ **OS map:** Explorer OL6 *English Lakes – South-western area*

▶ **Local attractions:** High Close Estate and Arboretum

▷ **THE PUBS:** Old Dungeon Ghyll, Great Langdale. Try also: New Dungeon Ghyll, Sticklebarn

▶ **Timing tip:** Check and check again the timing of the buses to and from Langdale.

The route up towards Stickle Tarn

Old Dungeon Ghyll

Pike of Stickle

Old Dungeon Ghyll to Pavey Ark

The best place to park is in the Old Dungeon Ghyll car park (£3 for the day). It's the first car park on the right and you pay in the hotel. The bus will also drop you off at the pub. From the back of the car park, there's a wooden gate leading to a field. Go through it and turn left towards a gate on the far wall. Follow the boggy track to a wooden footbridge. Cross it and turn left through another gate into the car park at the National Trust-owned Sticklebarn. (The National Trust campsite here must be among one of the most scenic in Britain.) Walk through the car park and in front of the public toilets, following a little path to the left. Walk through another gate and you'll see the National Trust sign to Stickle Ghyll.

This exciting path leads up the side of Stickle Ghyll, a fast-flowing stream fed by Stickle Tarn, our first destination of the day. With the roar of the ghyll (especially when in spate), it's a lively walk up.

At **A** NY291068, cross the wooden footbridge and continue uphill to the right of the ghyll. The footpath is very clear. In recent years there's been a clean path for most of the way. Work on the path has been undertaken to stop erosion, which was becoming quite a problem. Towards the top of the ghyll it gets a bit steep and you may need to put a hand down, but before you know it the expanse of Stickle Tarn opens up before you with the impressive mass of Pavey Ark looming above. Behind you Lingmoor Fell rises up, seeming greater than its relatively diminutive (for this area at least) height of 469 metres. Beyond that, the south-eastern Lake District and the Coniston fells (see Walk 3) can be seen in all their glory. You should also be able to make out Windermere on a clear day.

When you arrive at Stickle Tarn, you'll see a dam to the left. This was constructed in 1838 to provide a steady supply of water for the residents below. However, it's the

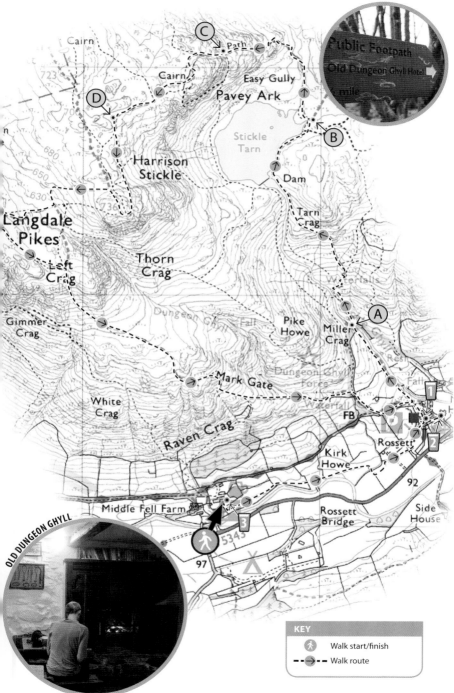

Cairn

Cairn

C Path

Easy Gully

Pavey Ark

D

Harrison
Stickle

Stickle
Tarn

B

Dam

Tarn
Crag

723

680

650

630

736

Langdale
Pikes

Left
Crag

Thorn
Crag

Waterfalls

Gimmer
Crag

Dungeon Ghyll Fall

Pike
Howe

Miller
Crag

A

Dungeon Ghyll
Force

Mark Gate

White
Crag

Raven Crag

Waterfalls

FB

Kirk
Howe

Rossett

92

Middle Fell Farm

3

5345

97

Rossett
Bridge

Side
House

Public Footpath
Old Dungeon Ghyll Hotel
¼ mile

OLD DUNGEON GHYLL

KEY

Walk start/finish

Walk route

Sun illuminating Raw Pike

A raging Stickle Ghyll

fell in the foreground that dominates the attention. Pavey Ark rises up to 700 metres in front of you in a pleasingly pyramidal shape. This huge cliff face is popular with climbers attacking various gullies, but it's Jack's Rake that holds most attention. We're going up the right side of Pavey Ark to the summit, but you should be able to make out a large scar that descends diagonally from top left to bottom right. This is a fairly hairy Grade

The silhouetted Langdale Pikes from Blea Tarn

1 scramble that's very exposed in parts (it's a long drop down). Most of the scramble is protected within the scar but there is one 'bad step' in particular that requires a head for heights and a sure footing. Although it's classed as Grade 1, many people still wear a rope for security plus a helmet. In wet conditions it can be treacherous – there have been fatalities on Jack's Rake. The British Mountaineering Council website has good

advice on scrambling this route
(thebmc.co.uk).

Our path up Pavey Ark was
named by Wainwright as the
North Rake (despite being the
eastern aspect). It is a fairly
straightforward, if strenuous,
hike up to the summit but will
require some hands on rocks at
the beginning. An experienced
hillwalker should have no
problem. To get there, walk
around the eastern end of the
tarn. In wet weather the area

A steadying hand needed near the top of Stickle Ghyll

immediately around the tarn maybe very
boggy – you'll be pleased you wore boots.
At **B** 🕙 **NY289077**, the path forks. Take the
left fork that rises up towards the eastern
side of Pavey Ark. There's a clear path that
leads to the bottom of the eastern buttress.
The trickiest and ever-so-slightly scrambly
bit is here, but it is reasonably easy. Once
up, the gap can be seen with a clear path
rising up. It's a fun little section, and one for

taking your time over and drinking in the
views. About half way up, at the top of what's
known as Easy Gully at **C** 🕙 **NY286080** – a
scramble up to the left from the bottom of
Jack's Rake – there's a great viewpoint.

Keep on climbing until the walking
flattens out a touch. Curve a little around to
the left and you'll see the rocky summit of
Pavey Ark. There's no cairn at the top, but the
views – wow!

Pike of Stickle from near Old Dungeon Ghyll

Pavey Ark to Old Dungeon Ghyll

From the top of Pavey Ark you should be able to see Harrison Stickle. Stickle, incidentally, means a hill with a prominent rocky top. At 736 metres, Harrison Stickle is also the high point of the day. From the south-west end of Pavey Ark's summit, you should be able to see the path leading to Harrison Stickle. It's tricky navigation here

Great Langdale from the top of Pavey Ark

if the cloud is down, however, as the rocks make the path unclear. There are a series of cairns that once you pick up, will lead you west above the steep drop towards Stickle Tarn. The route does descend slightly. Once you get to around **D** ◷ NY281077, you should be able to pick up the clear path south and up an increasing incline to Harrison Stickle. The path weaves around the eastern side of the summit, before turning up to the summit proper. There are two cairns on the top, with the northern one being the highest (if you want to touch it!). Is there a better place for a cheese sandwich in the Lake District?

There are several routes off Harrison Stickle. We want to descend directly west from the summit. Being wary of the incredibly steep drop to the south and south-western aspects, walk to the western side of the summit and you should see the path zigzagging down towards boggy crossroads below.

Walking up Harrison Stickle

When you get to the crossroads, and before scrambling up to Pike of Stickle, it's worth making a mental note of the return trip. It's common here to be enticed down below Thorn Crag, along Dungeon Ghyll. There is a path, but it's steep and not as pleasant or as maintained as the path we're taking, which is just around Loft Crag and down the ridge below.

Pike of Stickle juts up proudly towards the sky and stands as a sentry to the fells beyond it. The cliffs down to Mickleden Beck, 600 metres below, give the whole fell a drama rarely matched even up here.

Walk along the clear path towards Pike of Stickle that rises gently, or take a compass bearing. As you arrive at the foot of the pike, there are a couple of ways to scramble up to the top and it's a matter of picking your way through the jumble. You may need to use your hands in a couple of places, but the top is wide enough for a few people and a large cairn. Once up the views are vast, especially looking south and east, while to the north, the larger fells, often in the shadows, take on a rather menacing aspect.

We begin our descent from Pike of Stickle, but instead of returning along the same path, stay up on the shallowly undulating ridge south-east towards the peaked summit

LANGDALE AXE FACTORY

Pike of Stickle was one of the most important areas of Neolithic stone axe production in Europe. Among the diverse strata of the scree slopes below it, towards Mickleden Beck, is a layer of greenstone – a hard volcanic rock, perfect for a stone axe. There's evidence of sites all over Great Langdale, but this fell revealed the most prolific activity. It's believed that axes were traded around Britain and Ireland during the period between 3800 and 2600BC. Langdale axes can be seen in the Kendal Museum, the Tullie House Museum and Art Gallery in Carlisle, as well as the British Museum. Of all the Neolithic axes found in the UK, about 27 per cent come from Langdale.

Sticklebarn

New Dungeon Ghyll

of Loft Crag. Below and to the right of Loft Crag is Gimmer Crag, a popular spot for climbing. We're skirting around to the left of the crag (unless you want to bag it as well) and then down in the dip below along a well-maintained route. The descent starts at a huge cairn and then heads between two prominent buttresses before opening out onto a wide, grassy ridge. The direction is clear, and follows the path, increasingly rocky, back down towards Sticklebarn. There is a bit of Dungeon Ghyll to negotiate – take care when it's very high. Through a gate and then you're back to the route you first took and **Sticklebarn**, the National Trust pub.

PUB INFORMATION

 STICKLEBARN
Great Langdale, LA22 9JU
015394 37356 • nationaltrust.org.uk •(has campsite)
Opening hours: 11-9 (11 Fri & Sat).

 NEW DUNGEON GHYLL
Great Langdale, LA22 9JX
015394 37213 • dungeon-ghyll.co.uk • 🏕
Opening hours: 11-11; 12-10.30 Sun

 OLD DUNGEON GHYLL
Great Langdale, LA22 9JY
odg.co.uk • 015394 37272 • 🏕
Opening hours: 11-11; 11-10.30 Sun

This is a nice little place to relax in front of the fire and play a board game. It serves good food and real ale. Also near here is the **New Dungeon Ghyll**, where there's the Walker's Bar that has a couple of handpumps.

The choice of pubs however, has to be *Good Beer Guide* regular the **Old Dungeon Ghyll**, one of the classic hillwalking pubs countrywide. As a hotel in the early 1900s it was sold to Professor GM Trevelyan who then gave it to the National Trust. A 'Climber's Bar' was opened in 1949, where it remains today (albeit now called the Hikers' Bar). It's set in old cow stalls (and looking around you can still see them), and is a lively place at the end of a good day of walking, particularly so when there's live music (first Wednesday of the month) and occasional open mic nights. Climbing heroes Joe Brown, Don Whillans, Ian MacNaught-Davis, Chris Bonington and Ian Clough have all drank in the bar or given talks here. It's a fun place, but they take their beer seriously: there were nine handpumps on when I visited, plus a collection of Good Beer Guides dating back to the 1980s on a shelf above the old log-fired range. The view from the beer garden is fantastic. This is a brilliant pub.

Scafell Pike

The highest mountain in England, three fantastic pubs, a brewery and a walk around the birthplace of British climbing; yep, you're set for a great day's walking. Yet Scafell Pike is often derided for the relative banality of its peak and the sheer number of walkers, including many 'Three Peakers', who trudge up to its summit. But that's to miss the point. Yes, the summit is little more than a boulder field, but this route is one full of intrigue and excitement: narrow mountainside paths, thigh-cramping ascents and vertiginous descents. We leave from the Wasdale Head Inn, one of the most important places in British climbing history, to climb to the summit ridge. A circuitous route home takes us below some of the cliffs those brave pioneers first climbed around 140 years ago.

▶ **Start/finish:** Wasdale Head Village Green car park

▶ **Access:** Car/taxi only. Car hire is available from Co-wheels car club at Oxenholme train station.

▶ **Distance:** 7 miles (11km)

▶ **Ascent:** 3,028ft (923m)

▶ **Duration:** 4-6 hours

▶ **Fitness:**

▶ **Navigation:** ✪ ✪ ✪

▶ **OS map:** Explorer OL6 The English Lakes – South-western area

▶ **Local attractions:** England's highest mountain, Wast Water and the smallest church in England, St Olaf's at Wasdale Head

▶ **THE PUBS:** Wasdale Head Inn, Wasdale; Strands Inn, Nether Wasdale; Hardknott Bar & Cafe at the Woolpack Inn, Boot

▶ **Timing tip:** Hardknott Pass, one route to the start, is extremely steep and can be treacherous if it's icy.

A steep descent from the summit of Scafell Pike

Looking up to Lingmell at the start

Firstly, a few words of warning. The weather up here is wildly unpredictable, even in summer or when the day seems a fine one from the pub at the start. Navigation is also challenging on the summit when the cloud is down. There are some small scrambly bits, including the 'Bad Step' on the Corridor Route back down. There are good handholds, but this is not for the inexperienced hillwalker. You will need a map, compass and the knowledge of how to take a bearing. For those suitably prepared, however, this is an exhilarating challenge and the stunning views from the summit, on a clear day, reward you well.

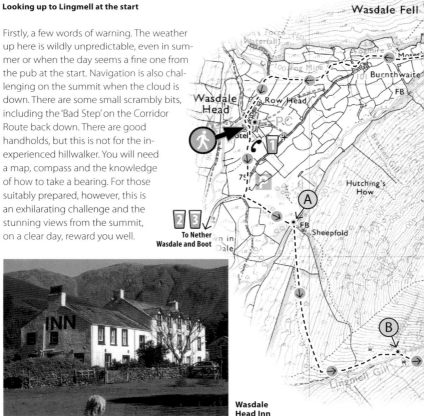

Wasdale Head Inn

Wasdale Head Inn to Scafell Pike

To get to the 978-metre summit of England's highest mountain we're taking one of the shortest routes, a steep but beautiful route up by Lingmell Gill, commonly known as the Hollow Stones route. The longer return walk is back down the celebrated Corridor Route towards Styhead Tarn and then back above Lingmell Beck under Great Gable. Scafell Pike is part of a hugely complex jumble of mountains, crags, fords, gills and pikes formed over 443 million years ago from igneous rock (cooled volcanic lava). Before the mid 1800s Sca Fell to the south-west of Scafell Pike was thought to be higher of the two, and undeniably

OLD PHOTO, WASDALE HEAD

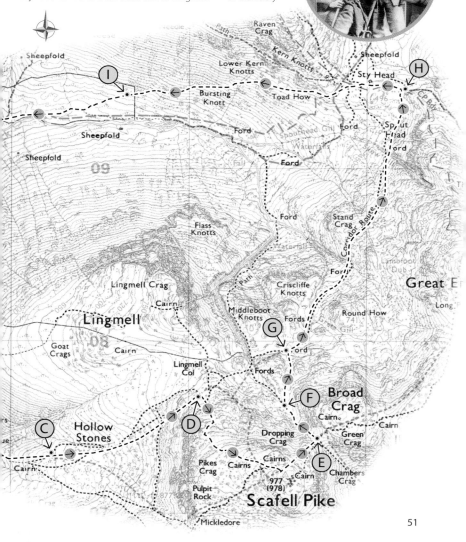

Mist hanging over Wast Water

looks like it, even from the summit of Scafell Pike (the reason the pike is attributed as such). Incidentally, the word 'Scafell' is pronounced 'Scawfell', and indeed this was the original spelling.

One final thought before starting is that there's a river crossing at NY195074. This can be tricky when the river's in spate. There may be better places above and below the crossing when the water is gushing, but crossing a river in spate is very dangerous.

Nomenclature sorted, warning given, sandwich packed, let's get moving. There are two car parks nearby, both run by the National Trust and there are public toilets at both spots. The Lake Head car park is the

first you'll get to, while the Wasdale Head Village Green car park is nearer to the pub at the end of the walk and therefore we'll start the route here. If you are setting off from the Lake Head car park, follow the signs to meet up with the main path a short way up Lingmell Gill.

From the Village Green car park, walk briefly along the road back towards Wast Water, until the road curves around to the right. A signpost is marked: 'Scafell Pike via Lingmell 2½ miles'. That doesn't seem too far, until you remember there are more than 800 metres of climbing.

Follow the sign across the field and over the wooden bridge at **A** ⊗ NY189081.

Lingmell Beck

Turn right through the gate and start the rocky ascent around Lingmell. As you climb, the views over Wast Water open up: it's one of the most spectacular places in the Lake District.

Wast Water, almost three miles long and 258ft deep, was scooped out by glaciation and is the deepest lake in England. The surface of the lake is around 200ft above sea level, but the bottom is 50ft below sea level. On a still day the Screes on the far side of the lake, that you'll have seen driving down, reflect perfectly in the water.

The sensitive and squeamish may wish to skip this paragraph, but it's an interesting story. In 1976 Margaret Hogg was killed by her husband after she attacked him at their home in Surrey. He wrapped her up in a carpet, tied it to a concrete block, drove to Wast Water and threw her in. The body however settled at only 110ft and, because of the lack of oxygen, remained well preserved. During the search for a missing student in 1983, Margaret Hogg's remains were found and her husband served four years for manslaughter. On a brighter note, mischievous divers put a gnome garden at the bottom complete with a picket fence. It has since been removed.

Crossing Lingmell Beck

As the path reaches Lingmell Gill, it turns east and follows the gill through the valley, with Lingmell Fell high above you on the left, and the foreboding crags of Sca Fell on the right. At **B** 🔄 NY195074 there's a crossing over the beck. In times

of heavy rain or meltwater it can be deep and sometimes crossing here isn't possible. In which case try either higher or lower for a more suitable crossing, but never cross unless you're absolutely sure there's no danger. Once you're over the beck, continue following this lovely path higher into the mountain complex. Soon you'll see Scafell Pike's western crags. As the ground flattens out slightly there's a fork in the path at around **C** 🔄 NY202073. The right-hand fork heads towards Mickledore col, another route to the Scafell Pike summit that is steeper and more challenging, requiring some scrambling over rather unpleasant scree.

Be sure to head left here and follow the easier route to the summit. Walk through the boulder field known as Hollow Stones and then zigzag up to Lingmell Col. At the col, **D** 🔄 NY210076, there's a junction. Going straight you'd pick up the Corridor Route that we'll join after summiting, but now turn right and uphill along the rough and rocky path. There's a number of cairns up here to follow, but probably too many, so don't rely on

The Northern Fells from the slopes of Scafell Pike

these alone as people can end up jumping onto a different path by blindly following cairns. As the ground flattens out on the wide summit you'll need to take a compass bearing, especially if you are in poor weather, as it can get very disorientating up here. If it's clear you'll have to rise a bit more before you see the large summit cairn at 978 metres. East of the summit cairn is a series of stone shelters, useful for a sandwich stop.

From the summit many of the great fells of the Lake District can be seen. Immediately to the east is Broad Crag (in the direction we're going next) and also in the far distance Blencathra and Helvellyn. To the south-east are Crinkle Crags and the Old Man of Coniston. To the south-west Sca Fell dominates the view, with Wast Water below it to the right. More to the west is Yewbarrow, which is directly behind the Wasdale Head Inn. To the north-west is Pillar and Kirk Fell, while to the north is the pleasingly mountain-shaped mass of Great Gable. On an exceptionally clear day you can see Snowdon in Wales and Slieve Donard, 111 miles away in County Down, Northern Ireland. The Ordnance Survey used the triangulation between these two mountains and Scafell Pike in the 1826 Principal Triangulation of Britain. Mind you, surveyors had to camp for much of the summer up here before they could get a clear observation.

Scafell Pike to Wasdale Head

From the summit cairn, we need to wind down to the col between Scafell Pike and Broad Crag at **E** 🕓 **NY217074**. There is a path, but it's very rocky and often not discernible. A couple of cairns from the summit suggest a route, but even in fair weather take a compass bearing to the col. As the path get steeper a jumble of routes zigzag tightly down to the col.

Once at the col, turn left and descend steeply north-west for a couple of hundred metres until the path forks at **F** 🕓 **NY215076**. Take the right fork heading directly north: it's important not to miss this turning. The path is fairly clear as it curves slightly down to the right. At **G** 🕓 **NY215079** you'll meet another path – this is the Corridor Route. Turn right on to it and follow it north-east for almost two kilometres. The Corridor Route is an exciting path with dramatic views that leads down to Styhead Tarn. As warned there's a bedrock 'Bad Step', at NY218085 above Greta Gill, which requires some down climbing. It should be fairly straightforward for an experienced hillwalker, but there have been some falls here. It's important not to start

Scafell Pike summit trig point

The pub in sight! Descending above Lingmell Beck

descending Greta Gill, especially in poor weather, as there's no way around it.

Once down the bedrock step it's an easy jaunt, mostly downhill, to the junction with the bridleway at **H** 🕐 NY221094. There are some becks to cross, but they are rarely impassable. At the junction, turn left and follow the clear path until you get to the stretcher box. Here you can head north to Styhead Tarn, however, we're heading west back to the pub!

Follow the path that goes left of the stretcher box. As you'll see from the map, there are two paths back down to Wasdale. We're staying up and taking the one that gently descends through Bursting Knott. It's the clearer path, but if you find yourself descending quite rapidly, you're probably heading down to Lingmell Beck. This is fine, but not as scenic.

As you head down this sometimes-rocky path, look back up Great Gable from around **I** 🕐 NY206094, and you should be able to see Napes Needle, a fantastic rock pinnacle. It was first climbed in 1886 by Walter Parry Haskett Smith and was made famous in photographs by the climbing and photography siblings the Abraham Brothers back in the 1890s and early 1900s. Some of their photographs can be seen in the Wasdale Head Inn.

The path now descends to the beck, and the Wasdale Head Inn can clearly be seen. Follow the signs back along the boggy path, past the farm at Burnthwaite, and take the right-hand path. Turn left at Mosedale Beck, past the world's most scenic stone bridge, and into the 🍺 **Wasdale Head Inn**.

This remarkable pub and hotel is often cited as the birthplace of climbing. It's certainly up there with the Clachaig Inn in the Highlands of Scotland (see Walk 12) and the Pen-y-Gwryd in Snowdonia (see Walk 18) in the annals of climbing history. The bar is named after Will Ritson, the first landlord of the inn. He was, to say the least, a colourful character, described on the Wasdale Head Inn's website as a huntsman, wrestler, farmer, fellsman, guide and raconteur. In short, the kind of guy you'd like to drink a pint with. He also inspired an annual competition called 'The World's Biggest Liar', where people are asked to spin the best yarns. It's held every November in the Bridge Inn, Stanton. Storytellers come from around the world to take part.

Ritson retired in 1879, just as the golden age of British climbing was about to begin, but he would have witnessed an increasing interest in the climbing of the fells around the Wasdale Head. The newly formed climbing fraternity, often from the middle

Woolpack Inn **Strands Inn**

and upper classes, would descend on the hotel. Walter Parry Haskett Smith and after him Owen Glynne Jones, star of some of the Abraham Brothers photographs in the hotel, were among the biggest names in the sport. Owen Glynne Jones, who often called himself the 'Only Genuine Jones', would perform stunts around the hotel. A well-known photograph of two climbers outside on the barn still hangs in the hotel. William Wordsworth, Charles Dickens and Samuel Taylor Coleridge, who scrambled up Scafell Pike in 1802, all stayed at the inn also.

Amongst the dozens of fascinating climbing photos and memorabilia around the hotel there are also photographs and paintings of Joss Naylor MBE, a local

resident who has been described as our greatest living athlete. As a fell runner he perhaps hasn't received the acclaim he deserves. He was born at Wasdale Head in 1936 and is still a regular face around here (this author met him in the Wasdale Head Inn on one occasion).

The second featured pub is a 20 minute drive away but well worth the trip. The **Strands Inn**, CAMRA Pub of the Year 2016 for Western Cumbria, is a delightful place with fantastic views over Wast Water and the Screes. It's a cosy, warming place run by friendly owners Mark and Lesley Corr. The Strands Brewery is also well regarded and has won plenty of awards for its many beers, including 'Errrmmm', a bitter named after the fact that they weren't very good at naming beers in the early days. There are now more than 30 styles, with half a dozen handpumps (more soon) and plenty of bottles. It's a great place.

The final recommendation, where this author stayed, is a little further away in Boot, Eskdale. The **Hardknott Bar & Cafe at the Woolpack Inn** is one of the most well-known Lake District pubs. It's a friendly place, with a good menu and modern rooms. The beer selection is superb, from local cask ales to the latest craft beers in the fridge and there are wood-burning stoves across two rooms. It's a convivial place to stay.

PUB INFORMATION

WASDALE HEAD INN
Wasdale Head, CA20 1EX
019467 26229 • wasdale.com •
Opening hours: 11-11; 12-10.30 Sun

STRANDS INN
Nether Wasdale, CA20 1ET
019467 26237 • strands-brewery.co.uk •
Opening hours: 11-11; 11-10.30 Sun

HARDKNOTT BAR & CAFE AT THE WOOLPACK INN
Boot, Eskdale, CA19 1TH
019467 23230 • woolpack.co.uk •
Opening hours: 9-11

Keswick circular

Cat Bells is one of the most popular fells to clamber up in the Lake District, and understandably so, as it can be ascended with relative ease and the views from the top are stunning. Before the climb up Cat Bells, however, this walk is a tranquil meander around Derwent Water, one of the most visited and photographed of England's lakes: it's beautiful. In summer launches and canoes cause ripples across the lake, while in winter an ethereal mist often swirls over the water. The lake, surrounded by high fells, has attracted artists and eccentrics, writers and sportspeople. You may also recognise it from a scene in *Star Wars Episode VII: The Force Awakens*, just with fewer X-Wings. Derwent Water has been a muse and an inspiration, and this route certainly makes the most of it. Arriving back in Keswick after this long and satisfying walk we're rewarded with two great pubs.

▶ **Start/finish:** Theatre by the Lake, Keswick

▶ **Access:** Regular buses from Penrith and Oxenholme. Car hire is available from Co-wheels car club at Oxenholme train station.

▶ **Distance:** 8.5 miles (14km)

▶ **Ascent:** 1,482ft (452m)

▶ **Duration:** 3.5-5 hours

▶ **Fitness:**

▶ **Navigation:**

▶ **OS map:** Explorer OL4 *The English Lakes – Northwestern area*

▶ **Local attractions:** Derwent Water, Cumberland Pencil Museum, Castlerigg Stone Circle, Keswick Museum and Art Gallery, Theatre by the Lake

▷ **THE PUBS:** Dog & Gun, Wainwright, both Keswick

▶ **Timing tip:** This walk could be shortened by catching a ferry part of the way, but check the timetables first.

The view towards Maiden Moor

Keswick to Lodore

We start at the brilliant Theatre by the Lake, also the venue for the thoroughly enjoyable Keswick Mountain Festival held in June. From the Theatre, walk south down towards the landing stages and along this popular stretch of lakeside path. The first destination is Friar's Crag, a little, wooded crag that presents one of Lakeland's best views. Continue along the wide path, and as it forks take the right-hand route that is clearly signposted to Friar's Crag.

Having paused to soak in the wonderful views from Friar's Crag (see box on page 60), return to the main path by cutting across by the John Ruskin memorial, through a wooden gate and around the top of the beach. Jump across the footbridges heading inland. The path curves around to the right and a wooden walkway lifts you above the mud below. At the junction at **A** NY269220 turn right past Stable Hills Cottage and back to the lakeside.

As the footpath weaves around Calfclose Bay don't miss a remarkable sculpture by artist Peter Randall-Page at the water's edge, **B** NY268215. It's known as the Hundred

The Hundred Year Stone

Year Stone and was placed here in 1995, marking the centenary of the National Trust.

The path turns a little wet here (you'll be grateful for waterproof boots), but a footbridge crosses the worst of it. The route now nears Borrowdale Road, and as it does there's a steep step up. At the road you'll see a pavement on the right. Follow that along the road a short while until some stone steps head down to a jetty. Continue left along the water's edge until you get to Kettlewell Car Park. Canoes and paddleboards often launch here.

Cross the road here and you'll see a footpath running against a wall. A fingerpost reads 'Lodore ½m'. This goes through some pleasant woodland and comes out just above Lodore Falls Hotel, with an unfortunate couple of hundred metres of road walking.

Islands of Derwent Water in the morning mist

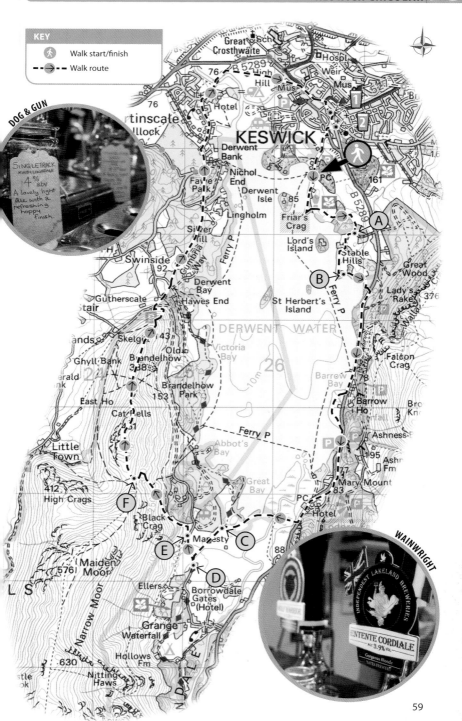

KEY

🚶 Walk start/finish

- -➤- - Walk route

DOG & GUN

SINGLETRACK
JOSEPH LONSDALE
4% abv
A lovely light
ale with a
refreshing
hoppy
finish.

Great
Crosthwaite

Hospl
B 5289
Weir
Mus
High
Hill
Mus

Hotel

KESWICK

Derwent
Bank

Nichol
End
PC
161
Faw
Park
Derwent
Isle
85
B 5289
Lingholm
Friar's
Crag
A
Silver
Hill
Lord's
Island
Stable
Hills
Great
Wood
Swinside
92
Cumbria Way
Ferry P
Derwent
Bay
B
Ferry P
Lady's
Rake
376
Gutherscale
Hawes End
St Herbert's
Island
tair
DERWENT WATER
Skelg
43
Victoria
Bay
26
Falcon
Crag
Ghyll Bank
38
Old
Brandelhow
28
erald
24
153
Barrow
Bay
78
ands
Brandelhow
Park
Barrow
Ho
Bro
Kn
East Ho
Ferry P
Ashness
Cat ells
Abbot's
Bay
P
P
Little
Town
195
Ash
Fm
412
High Crags
Great
Bay
Mary Mount
83
PC
F
Hotel
Black
Crag
Majesty
C
E
88
D
WAINWRIGHT
Maiden
576
Moor
Ellers
Borrowdale
Gates
(Hotel)
Grange
Waterfall
L
S
Hollows
Fm
630
Nitting
Haws
stle
ok

WAINWRIGHT

Independent Lakeland Breweries

ENTENTE CORDIALE
ALC 3.9% VOL
Gorgeous Blonde
YATES BREWERY

Raised platform over the boggy outlet of the River Derwent

Lodore to Hause Gate

Back on a pavement, walk past the hotel and buildings on the right until a wide path heading west opens up. There are lovely views here across Borrowdale.

Cross the bridge that arches over the River Derwent, a river that rises out of Sprinkling Tarn near Scafell Pike, and follow the path, often on a raised platform, through the open land. A few paths crisscross this section. You are aiming for a gate at **C** NY254186 and then to follow a path that rises and dips diagonally south-west. Through the gate you are now on the Cumbria Way. This clearly continues to a quiet road at **D** NY251182.

A signpost at the road reads 'Cat Bells'. Turn right and you'll see a bridleway that ascends north-west. Jump on to this bridleway at **E** NY250185 and follow it up above the plantation. When the path forks be sure to stay left and continue increasingly steeply uphill until you reach the top of the ridge and a cross of paths at **F** NY244192.

FRIAR'S CRAG AND THE ISLANDS OF DERWENT WATER

A slate memorial to the art critic, painter and philanthropist John Ruskin has been erected here with the words: 'The first thing I remember…was being taken by my nurse to the brow of Friar's Crag.' Ruskin described the view from Friar's Crag as one of the most beautiful in Europe. He spent much of his life in the Lake District and a visit to his home, Brantwood above Coniston, is highly recommended (see box on page 60).

It is thought that Friar's Crag was named after monks who used it as a launching place for a boat to get to St Herbert's Island. The island is named after a priest who made it his home in the 7th century and it became a place of pilgrimage. The remains of a 14th-century chapel can be seen on the island. It was also the inspiration for Owl Island in Beatrix Potter's book, *The Tale of Squirrel Nutkin*.

The nearest island to Friar's Crag, and seen directly east, is Derwent Island, which was bought by a Joseph Pocklington in 1778. He built a house, a fort, gothic boathouse and a mock stone circle. During annual regattas he used the fort for mock battles, firing his cannons. Today, the island is still inhabited and is open to the public just five days a year.

The National Trust now looks after the four islands on Derwent Water and Friar's Crag itself was given to the National Trust in 1920 as a memorial to Canon Rawnsley, one of the three founders of the organisation.

Mist hanging over Maiden Moor

Hause Gate to Keswick

From Hause Gate there's a clear path that rises gently up onto Cat Bells at 451 metres. You'll likely start bumping into more people here – this is one of the most popular fells in the Lake District thanks to its relative ease of access and impressive viewpoint over Derwent Water. If you've seen it from the beginning of the walk, you'll know how appealing it is. Lake District writer Alfred Wainwright (see box overleaf) wrote of it: 'It is one of the great favourites, a family

fell where grandmothers and infants can climb the heights together, a place beloved. Its popularity is well deserved, its shapely topknot attracts the eye offering a steep but obviously simple scramble.'

Below to the left is the impressive Newlands Valley with Causey Pike and Grisedale Pike beyond it. This seemingly serene view largely hides the industrial heritage of the area. If you'd have continued over Hause Gate, down the bridleway the other side, the remnants of lead mines under Yewthwaite Comb can be seen. A number

The southern end of Derwent Water

Rising up to the ridge

of the shafts remained open for many years after the mines shut down in the 1890s, but most are now closed up.

Whether alchemists got in on the act we don't know, but as well as the lead mines, Newlands Valley was also home to gold and silver mines over centuries. The Goldscope mine, which closed in the late 19th century, operated from at least the 16th century, but it was mostly lead and copper that was extracted, and in huge amounts. Yet the heritage of the area goes back even further, with the remains of settlements dating back to the Bronze Age. Evidence of Vikings, as all across the Lake District, is apparent too from the Old Norse names. Between AD800-1100, Vikings lived all around. Nearby High Seat, a 608-metre fell, for example, is named 'seat'

meaning 'summer pasture'. 'Thwaite', for instance in Rosthwaite (a little village just a couple of kilometres from where you stand), means clearing. Fell means mountain from the Old Norse of 'fjall'. Similarly, beck, dale, howe, ghyll, pike, seat and tarn all derive from Old Norse words. Cat Bells, however, remains a mystery; perhaps it is a distortion of 'Cat Bields' meaning the den of a wild cat.

With this in mind, time to press on to 'cheese farm', also known as Keswick. The route ahead is simple and even includes a mild scramble. It's a lovely sight seeing the path heading down along the ridge. As it gets steeper on the final brow it zigzags its way down to the road. There's been quite a bit of erosion here so follow the clearest route - it comes out just to the right of the ridge. Once

Newlands Valley from Cat Bells

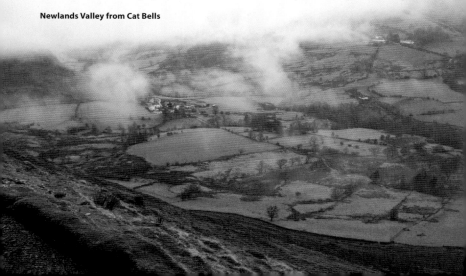

at the road, cross it and you'll see a path that continues downhill towards the woodland and a white house. Head down here and then go through the gate by the cattle grid and onto the path above the road. As the road curves around to the left, follow the path straight ahead; a sign shows 'Portinscale 1½ miles'. Despite being off the mountain there's still a fair way to get back into Keswick.

The clear path goes in and out of woodland before arriving at the Lingholm Estate where there is a cafe and gallery, the Lingholm Kitchen. Beatrix Potter, forever associated with the Lake District, spent nine summers at the estate in the 1800s and she based Mr McGregor's garden in *Peter Rabbit* on the kitchen gardens serving Lingholm mansion. Squirrel Nutkin also 'lived' in the Lingholm Woods you're walking through.

WAINWRIGHT'S WORLD

Alfred Wainwright (1907-1991) will be forever linked with the Lake District. The indefatigable walker produced seven famous pictorial guides to the Lakeland Fells, which are still essential guides to Lake District walking. The information packed into these beautifully illustrated books is quite astonishing. According to the Wainwright Society's website (wainwright.org.uk), seeing the Lake District for the first time, he wrote: 'I was totally transfixed, unable to believe my eyes. I had never seen anything like this. I saw mountain ranges, one after another, the nearer starkly etched, those beyond fading into the blue distance.

Rich woodlands, emerald pastures and the shimmering water of the lake below added to a pageant of loveliness, a glorious panorama that held me enthralled. I had seen landscapes of rural beauty pictured in the local art gallery, but here was no painted canvas; this was real. This was truth. God was in his heaven that day and I a humble worshipper'.

The 214 fells of the Lake District that are featured in Wainwright's books are now known as Wainwrights, with walkers bagging them as they would do Munros in Scotland. He also devised the hugely popular Coast to Coast Walk from St Bees to Robin Hood's Bay.

Stand-up paddleboarders on the River Derwent

Dog & Gun

Wainwright

An old sign directs you to Keswick another two miles away. You'll come out at Derwent Bank and a boatyard. Walk through the boatyard to the left until you come out on to the road that leads into Portinscale. Just after the cafe on the left, turn right, following a green sign showing a public footpath to Keswick. Go straight past Derwent Manor and continue until the road turns into a footpath just before a large footbridge over the River Derwent. Just after the bridge, turn right onto the fenced path that crosses the fields, with Keswick ahead of you. You'll come out at another bridge by the Cumberland Pencil Museum. Time to find the **Dog & Gun**. Walk along Main Street, going over the roundabout, until you get to Moot Hall, with the Tourist Information Centre on the ground floor. The Dog & Gun is down the road to the right.

After a tiring day on the hills, it's practically obligatory to order the goulash here with your pint. The Dog & Gun has long been a favourite among walkers and gets very busy. Despite a fairly recent refurbishment it retains its former character and has some old walking memorabilia on the walls. There's a fantastic collection of beers too. On my visit that included local beers from Kirkby Lonsdale Brewery, Keswick Brewing Co and Cumbrian Legendary Ales with the ever-available Loweswater Gold, the 2011 Champion Golden Ale of Britain. A CAMRA discount is given for card-carrying members.

Also welcoming for walkers (there's a pair of boots hanging outside that have completed the 214 'Wainwright' Fells) is the **Wainwright** further down Lake Road back towards the theatre. This is a place where any walker will feel at home. Prints and photographs of the fells are on the walls (including a signed print from the writer of this book's foreword, Alan Hinkes). Also on display are the spectacular line drawings of the fells by the lovely Mark Richards, whose eight-volume collection of *Lakeland Fellranger* books is the definitive modern guide to the fells of the Lake District. There's also a fantastic range of beers from local breweries including Fell, Tractor Shed, Tarn Hows and Strands (see page 56). Note the 'pictorial guide to our Lakeland ales' on the wall near the bar.

PUB INFORMATION

DOG & GUN
2 Lake Road, Keswick, CA12 5BT
017687 73463 • thedogandgunkeswick.co.uk
Opening hours: 11-11 (midnight Fri & Sat);
12-11 Sun

WAINWRIGHT
Lake Road, Keswick, CA12 5BZ
017687 44927 • thewainwright.pub
Opening hours: 11.30-11.30 (midnight Fri & Sat)

Malham to Settle

WALK
7

This walk has it all: geological wonders, exposed moorland, expansive scenery, an occasional hint of danger and some brilliant pubs. It features some of the best natural attractions in the Yorkshire Dales National Park, among them Malham Cove, Gordale Scar and Janet's Foss. It reads like a greatest hits and it's all within ten miles. The route starts out at the Malham National Park Centre and heads up through Gordale Scar, which requires a little bit of scrambling up a wet waterfall. It is short, but falling isn't an option. To avoid the scramble follow the signs out of Malham to Malham Cove and pick up the route there, knocking a couple of miles off the full distance. Be sure to visit Gordale Scar either way. Once you've puffed up the waterfall, it's a pleasant walk over to Malham Cove, past the little-visited Attermire Scar and into Settle. A shuttle service runs between Settle and Malham on Sundays and bank holidays in the summer otherwise you either need two cars or to take a five-mile taxi ride back to Malham It's very much worth the effort, though.

▶ **Start/Finish:** Malham National Park Centre

▶ **Access:** Two buses daily from Skipton to Malham. Bus number 881 connects Settle and Malham on summer Sundays and bank holidays.

▶ **Distance:** 10 miles (16km)

▶ **Ascent:** 1,811ft (552m)

▶ **Duration:** 4-6 hours

▶ **Fitness:** 👟👟

▶ **Navigation:** 🧭🧭

▶ **OS map:** Explorer OL2 – Yorkshire Dales – Southern & Western areas

▶ **Local attractions:** Malham Cove, Gordale Scar, Janet's Foss, Malham National Park Centre

▶ **THE PUBS:** Lister Arms, Malham; Talbot Arms, Settle; Hart's Head, Giggleswick. Try also: The Buck Inn, Malham.

▶ **Timing tip:** Returning from Settle to Malham needs some careful consideration if you're aiming to catch the bus.

Limestone pavement above Gordale

Malham to Malham Cove

Start out at the Malham National Park Centre on the road into Malham. There's a large car park that isn't obnoxiously priced and the centre itself has a small selection of maps and outdoor equipment if you've forgotten anything. There's also some interesting information about the Yorkshire Dales National Park. Here you need to decide whether you want to take the short scramble up the waterfall at Gordale Scar. It requires a slippery trot across some stepping stones before a short climb where you wouldn't want to slip. In short, if the thought

makes you a little nervous and you haven't done any scrambling before, head straight up the Pennine Way to Malham Scar. Also, if there's been a lot of rain or there's meltwater, the scramble may not be possible at all. Either way the start is the same.

From the Park Centre, walk into Malham. At the Buck Inn turn right across the bridge towards the Lister Arms, a marvellous little pub to visit on your return. The Pennine Way weaves to the left around the pub. If you're skipping the scramble, turn up here to follow the Pennine Way to Malham Cove (and skip the rest of this section). To get to Gordale Scar (a must-visit at some point anyway),

The lane to Gordale Scar

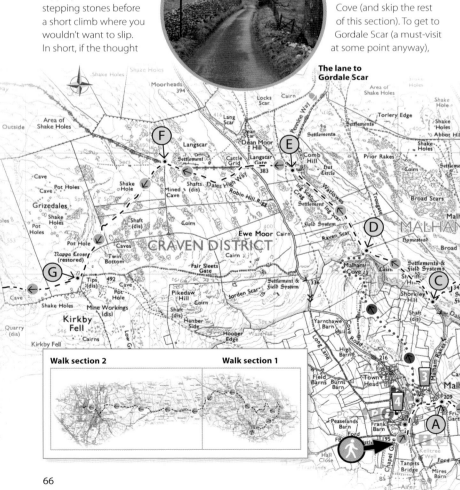

continue past the Youth Hostel and up Finkle Street. There's a partially restored sheep pinfold on the right. Any stray sheep were brought to this pinfold to be repatriated with the right farmer. Villages would often employ 'pinders' to keep an eye on the animals.

Keep walking along Gordale Lane, signposted to Gordale. It's a quiet lane, but take care nonetheless. At **A** SD903629 there's a sign for a permissive footpath that cuts out part of the road. It's not marked on the OS map. Go through the gate and follow the footpath that rises then descends back to the road (turn left back onto the road). As you rise up to the brow and begin the winding descent the nature of the landscape begins to change. Here there's no doubt why the rocky outcrops are known as scars. The violent geological action that wreaked devastation through the rock can be seen. It's particularly vivid at Janet's Foss. To get there head down to the bottom of the hill and just before the bridge, or two bridges

Looking up Gordale Scar

actually, a footpath descends off to the right. A National Trust sign is marked 'Janet's Foss, Malham Tarn Estate'. It's a short walk down and should not be missed. As you walk down the path you'll hear the roar of the water first, and then this magical little waterfall comes into view. An interpretation board tells the story of Janet, or Jennet, the queen of the local fairies, who lived in a cave behind the waterfall (foss means waterfall or force). This damp, shady spot has formed its own ecosystem; look out for wild garlic in spring.

KEY

🚶 Walk start/finish

- - → - - Walk route

•• ● •• Alternative route

Janet's Foss

Back up onto the lane, cross the bridge and turn left along the footpath towards Gordale Scar. This field is also a campsite and in summer there'll be dozens of tents. Here the true force of what water can do to the earth is clearly visible. It's impossible not to feel a little awestruck by the surroundings, especially on reading that it's a landscape formed over a period of more than 1.5 million years with three major glaciers covering Malham. Each time the resulting meltwater has carved its way through the limestone to create this spectacular chasm.

A quote on an interpretation board from watercolour artist Edward Dayes, published in 1805 (he committed suicide in 1804), sums up the scene, if a little dramatically, thus: '… every object conspires to produce one of the grandest spectacles in nature. The rocks dart their bold and rugged fronts to the heavens, and impending fearfully over the head of the spectator, seem to threaten his immediate destruction.' The famous painting by James Ward is equally dramatic, and some sensitive Victorians who hadn't seen it with their own eyes no doubt considered it to be the gates of hell on seeing the rendition.

As you walk into the ravine you'll see the lower waterfall before you. Take a judgement here on whether you fancy it. There are a couple of ways to proceed: up the right hand side or to the left of the principal waterfall. I found to the left up the central buttress the easiest route. The right hand side may look easier from below, but it requires some airy leaps of faith – not great when it's wet and slippery. Note that after heavy rain the approach is much more difficult and,

THE BUCK INN

Exposed limestone above Gordale Scar caused by a glacial retreat

frankly, probably isn't worth it. To get to the central buttress walk around to the right of the ravine and cross where you can in front of the central waterfall. There's often a weaker waterfall to the right. Hop across

the stones and then feel your way up the central buttress taking as small a step as possible. The good handholds have been worn by thousands of scramblers before you. It is short, but exciting. Soon you'll be at the

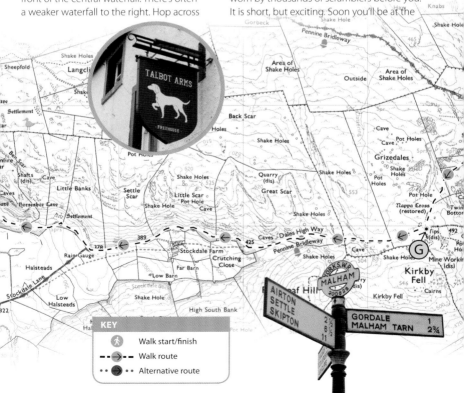

Walker on the path by Gordale Beck

next level where you'll see the spectacular waterfall plummeting through the rock to your right. Stay to the left of the main water until you see the stone steps that lead steeply out of the ravine. You'll have worked up a sweat by now but will have a big smile on your face.

Follow the path across the top until you reach a stone stile. Don't cross it, but turn left and walk along the wall briefly before cutting across the top of Gordale Scar back south. There's a clear path that follows the edge of the ravine. Admire some of the fantastical shapes formed on limestone pavement. The way is a little unclear here (and not marked on the map). Don't descend, instead follow the path west around the top of the cliffs and then back north until you see a north-south wall. Walk north beside the wall and you'll see a sign marked 'Stone stile 15 mts' on a wooden gate around **B** 🕙 SD910640, and sure enough there it is. Cross the wall and then cut diagonally north-west across the field towards the road. That's the trickiest bit of navigation over. At the road, walk left along it

for almost a kilometre – it's quiet but there are some blind corners. At **C** 🕙 SD902637 there's a large wooden stile and a sign marked Malham Cove, you'll also likely start bumping into more and more people. Follow the path until you see the splendour of Malham Cove's limestone pavement before you, one of the finest examples of it anywhere in the world. Walk down towards it and a gate with a fingerpost marked the Pennine Way.

Malham Cove to Settle

If you've come up the Pennine Way directly from Malham you'll have cut across the bottom of Malham Cove, appreciating its true arching grandeur, and climbed up to the west of its main face. Then walk across the top of the pavement to the fingerpost at **D** 🕙 SD897641.

Malham Cove's limestone pavement was formed by meltwater from glaciers at the end of the last ice age around 12,000 years ago. The cove itself was formed by a waterfall, and in December 2015 after Storm Desmond, the water returned briefly, falling 80 metres into

Malham Beck. The water usually runs down from Malham Tarn, 1.5 miles north of the cove, and then underground, appearing just to the east of the cove. Peregrine falcons have nested here since 1993.

After taking time to explore Malham Cove, continue north along the Pennine Way and north-west along Ing Scar. At **E** 🔍 **SD891648** the Pennine Way branches off north but we're taking the Dales High Way directly west towards Langscar Gate. Cross Cove Road and follow the signpost marked 'Byway, Cow Close, Langcliffe'. Here a wide track leads uphill onto the moor. Keep an eye out, however, for another sign at **F** 🔍 **SD881649** marked 'Pennine Bridleway, Stockdale Lane 2 miles', as this is our next destination. It's a mild uphill walk here. Keep an eye out for Nappa Cross, a medieval way-marker now restored. It's been written that monks may have met here for services.

Follow the wall after Nappa Cross to the T-junction of paths at **G** 🔍 **SD875639**. Follow the Dales High Way/Pennine Bridleway west down towards Stockdale Farm. It's a lovely stretch of the walk as the views to the west open up again. Half a kilometre after the entrance to the farm look out for a fingerpost that indicates 'FP

Settle 2' – only a couple of miles to the pub now! This stunning section of the route follows a path that leads under Attermire Scar. These limestone crags are replete with caves, including the Victoria Cave, which is about a kilometre north of the route beyond Attermire Scar. It was discovered in 1837, the year of Queen Victoria's coronation. Warning, there follows some words you wouldn't expect in a walking route in the Yorkshire Dales! In this cave explorers found 130,000-year-old remains of hippos, narrow-nosed rhinos, elephants and hyenas. Also found were the remains of a bear and an 11,000-year-old antler harpoon, indicating the earliest evidence of human occupation. Roman brooches, coins and pottery, including some from Africa, were also found here leading some archaeologists to believe there was a shrine of some sort.

Continue west along the Dales High Way. Some parts here are boggy until the path begins to climb up to above Settle. As the town comes into focus there's a steep, but clear, descent down to a lane. There'll be signs for the Pennine Bridleway to Settle. As you emerge off the path and onto the lane, turn left and follow Highway, then left again down Castle Hill and along the cobbles to

Fingerpost suggesting two miles to the pub

Lister Arms

Hart's Head Hotel

Cheapside, where you'll see the **1** **Talbot Arms Hotel** on the left.

The Talbot Arms has won several local CAMRA branch awards, including Pub of the Year in 2016. It's a friendly destination popular with families, walkers and locals. A stove heats one of the rooms and beyond is an adjoining room with pool table, dartboard and dominoes that is the home for several local leagues. The pub also has the largest beer garden in Settle. On handpump when I visited were beers from Bridgehouse, Leeds and Settle breweries.

The next nearest pub that regularly features in the *Good Beer Guide* is in Giggleswick, a 15-minute walk away. The **2** **Hart's Head Hotel** is a large place that still manages to feel cosy and lived in. The bar area has a real fire and a convivial atmosphere. This 18th-century coaching inn has a pool table and a full snooker table in the cellar. There's a pleasant beer garden out the back. It's popular with cyclists in particular. It was just about to change hands when I visited, but it's likely they'll keep the good selection of beer, which included Black Sheep and a couple of guests from nearby Settle and Dark Horse breweries. At any one time there are five handpumps serving real ale.

Back in Malham, the **3** **Lister Arms** is a beautifully looked after 17th-century coaching inn by the village green. Walking into the tiled entrance hall is a great feeling. There's a stone-flagged main bar, as well as a dining room. This is a Thwaites pub, but of the six handpumps, three are guest beers, usually local. Also worth a visit is the **4** **Buck Inn**; a sign reads: 'Muddy boots welcome'.

PUB INFORMATION

1 TALBOT ARMS
High Street, Settle, BD24 9EX
01729 823924 • talbotsettle.co.uk
Opening hours: 12-11

2 HART'S HEAD HOTEL
Belle Hill, Giggleswick, BD24 0BA
01729 822086 • hartsheadhotel.co.uk •
Opening hours: 12 (Tue-Fri)-11; 11.30-11 Sat; 12-11
Sun. Winter closing times apply.

3 LISTER ARMS
Gordale Scar Road, Malham, BD23 4BD
01729 830330 • listerarms.co.uk •
Opening hours: 8am-11

Try also:

4 BUCK INN
Cove Road, Malham, BD23 4DA
01729 830317 • thebuckmalham.co.uk •
Opening hours: 12-11 Mon-Sat; 12-10.30 Sun

Hart's Head Hotel

Arkengarthdale

Swaledale and the subsidiary dale of Arkengarthdale are all but dead-ends, with only vast moorland, impossibly green pastures and lonely lanes beyond. For walkers this means a wealth of places to enjoy the best of the Yorkshire Dales. This is a walk of two halves. The first section rises high above the villages of Grinton and Reeth, along the precipitous Fremington Edge, before descending down to Arkle Beck for a return riverside jaunt through woodland and farmland that has a completely different character. It's a fairly straightforward walk and short-ish (for this book at least), but there's nothing wrong with walking around what could be the most beautiful dale in Yorkshire with a couple of cosy pubs to finish.

▶ **Start/Finish:** Bridge Inn, Grinton

▶ **Access:** Regular buses between Richmond and Reeth also stop at Grinton

▶ **Distance:** 7.5 miles (12km)

▶ **Ascent:** 1,286ft (392m)

▶ **Duration:** 3-5 hours

▶ **Fitness:** 👢👢

▶ **Navigation:** 🧭🧭

▶ **OS Map:** Explorer OL30 *Yorkshire Dales – Northern & Central areas*

▶ **Local attractions:** Swaledale Museum, mountain biking

▶ **THE PUBS:** Bridge Inn, Grinton; Buck Inn, Reeth. Try also: Red Lion, Langthwaite; King's Arms, Black Bull, Reeth

View to Calver Hill across Arkengarthdale

Looking west from below Fremington Edge

Grinton to Storthwaite Hall

Our walk starts at the Bridge Inn that sits by a crossing of the River Swale. Around this bridge, which crosses one of the fastest running rivers in the country, formed the little village of Grinton, a word meaning 'green pasture' in Old English. The pub is opposite St Andrew's. This huge church is often called the Cathedral of the Dales, and is seemingly incongruous for such a small village until you realise that it once served much of Swaledale, as a wander around the churchyard browsing the tombstones attests. Bodies were carried from as far as Keld, 13 miles away at the western end of Swaledale, to be buried here. Parts of the 12th-century Norman church remain, but most of what you see today is from the 15th century.

From the pub, walk north over the 18th-century bridge at and towards Fremington along the path. On the left you'll pass the Dales Bike Centre, an excellent place to hire a bike to explore the many bridleways around here, but also a good spot for a coffee.

Take the first right in Fremington signposted Marrick and Hurst and then, after an old barn with a small sign reading 'AD Barn', turn left up the small lane and into High Fremington. No beating around the bush, there's a long uphill struggle now to

Fremington Edge, but take solace in the scenery and views that continue to improve as you ascend.

At the top of the lane turn left and then follow the lane around to the right and uphill. This weaving, wooded lane climbs and climbs towards the aptly named White House. By now the views should have taken your breath away as much as the ascent. Reeth is clearly seen below you and the rest of Swaledale beyond that. Rising above it is Calver Hill – any unnatural curves and bumps you can see are testament to the industry that once raged in this area. In particular lead mining during the 19th century left its mark in Swaledale, and as you look above you the quarries on Fremington Edge are evident. Arkengarthdale narrows to the north towards Langthwaite. We're in surprisingly remote country now, and places like Langthwaite are becoming more and more disconnected. No longer do three buses a day and a bank van make the short trip to the village. This route doesn't quite reach the village either, but there is a lovely little pub there, the **3** **Red Lion**, that doubles as the village shop.

The old road turns now into a rocky path. At **A** NZ044002, there's a turn-off to the White House. We're still going up. The track is rather a mess from here to the top; pick out a well-used path and follow it diagonally up until you reach the stone wall and a gate. The

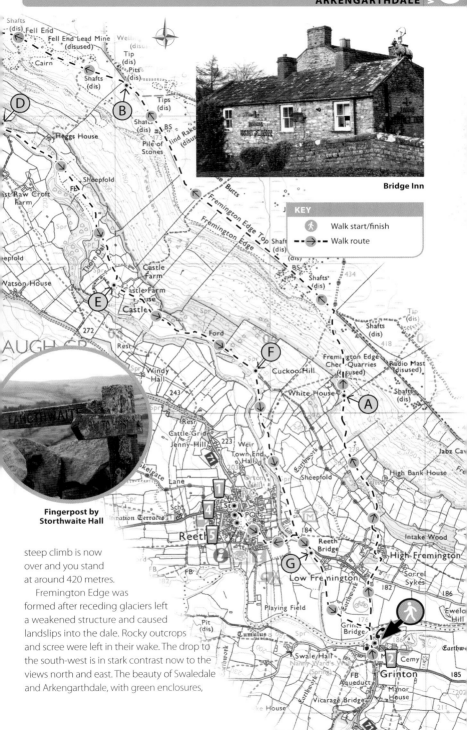

Bridge Inn

KEY

🚶 Walk start/finish

– – ➙ – – Walk route

**Fingerpost by
Storthwaite Hall**

steep climb is now
over and you stand
at around 420 metres.

Fremington Edge was
formed after receding glaciers left
a weakened structure and caused
landslips into the dale. Rocky outcrops
and scree were left in their wake. The drop
to the south-west is in stark contrast now to the
views north and east. The beauty of Swaledale
and Arkengarthdale, with green enclosures,

View over Arkengarthdale

lively brooks and stone cottages, is completely different from the expansive moorland to the north. Fremington Edge skirts Marrick Moor that is used, like many of the moors around here, for grouse shooting.

The principal view is spectacular. During the summer, the heather in bloom is an evocative sight, but for the rest of the year you'll find yourself admiring the ever-changing colours that shine upon Arkengarthdale. It has certainly attracted plenty of location scouts over the years, with scenes from *All Creatures Great and Small* being frequently filmed up here, among many others.

Bridge Inn

Go through the gate and turn left along the impressive stone wall. The footpath follows the wall until our descent through Fell End Lead Mine. It's usually boggy along this path and may require a bit of jumping over puddles. Count yourself lucky if you get to the end without wet feet.

The path continues to slowly climb, past a crossroads of footpaths to the high point of 473 metres, marked by a cairn. Continue a little further to a gate at **B** ◈ NZ031022 where a bridleway meets the path and begins its descent through Fell End Lead Mine. We're also heading down. Here, the pock holes of disused mines can be seen all around. There are also some disused shafts. Although the path is wide and there are small cairns that lead the way – don't stray too far from the track. Straight ahead you'll see the pleasingly named hamlet of Booze, although for the nearest pint it's to the Red Lion in Langthwaite. Also worth noting is that at the very end of the dale is the famous Tan Hill Inn, the highest pub in England.

The bridleway curves sharply back down into the valley and zigzags on a rocky descent towards Storthwaite Hall.

ARKENGARTHDALE LEAD MINING

The industrial heritage around here has a long history. Lead is thought to have been taken from the land for more than 1,000 years. A lead ingot was found in the 19th century with the name 'Hadrian' stamped on it, fuelling the belief that the Romans also mined here. Arkengarthdale's population has risen and fallen with the economy of the area. According to Margaret Batty's *A View of Arkengarthdale*, in 1831 there were 285 miners in the valley. This, however, proved to be a high point for the population, and a continuing fall in the price of lead resulted in many workers abandoning the dale. By the time of the 1851 census there were 254 miners and the decline continued. The last lead mine closed in 1914.

Derelict cottage in Arkengarthdale

Storthwaite Hall to Grinton

As you reach a house on your right at **C** ⊙ NZ018021, turn left and go on past the hall to follow the bridleway east and down to Arkle Beck. It meets a footpath on the northern side of the beck at a fantastic wooden footbridge at **D** ⊙ NZ022019. The path across the bridge can be taken back to Reeth, but the path on the northern side of the beck is more pleasant, if a little boggier.

From the bridge you'll see a small gate just a little further along by the beck. Walk down here and not up the bridleway that strays off to the left. From this point the footpath is often indistinct as it passes through broken walls, boggy copses and open farmland. However, if you keep an eye open when the path seems to disappear, you should quickly pick it up again. The route is also quite undulating with some short but steep sections and is sometimes a bit wet.

Castle Farm House is at **E** ⊙ NZ030008. A fingerpost points in the direction of the house and you'll see some yellow marks on walls to follow through the farmyard. It's fairly open along this part, but the path is just about worn enough to follow. Out of the farmyard another couple of yellow marks indicate the footpath through the stone wall and then across a couple of open fields and

right in front of a dilapidated, but somewhat photogenic, farmhouse. The famous round-horned Swaledale sheep are the only residents here these days.

The path drifts back towards the beck, and picks up the bridleway where the going is clearer. At **F** ⊙ NZ039002 the footpath splits off right again. You'll pass another barn with a big yellow arrow painted on it directing you across open fields. Head down to the fence in the southern corner of the field and head south to the west of the wall. The path again becomes clear and you'll see a fingerpost directing you towards Reeth. Pass another barn and you'll see the road in the distance.

Evening sun lights up Fell End

At the road, jump through the gate and cross the bridge over Arkle Beck and into Reeth. Follow the road around to the right, past Reeth Village Store, and up to the large village green.

Reeth is a lively village and busy with tourists in the summer. There are several cafes, galleries and shops. We however are more interested in the pubs, of which there are three.

The **Buck Hotel** is often featured in the *Good Beer Guide*. It's an 18th-century coaching inn that started off life as a tollgate before quickly becoming a place for respite. Today, the pub is popular with walkers, particularly those walking the Coast to Coast. There are two beamed rooms, one with a log fire in winter. Accommodation is available and the food is also well-liked. In the high season the bar has five handpumps operating with two of them reserved for guest ales; all the beers are from Yorkshire. There's also a regularly changing selection of five ciders, perfect for a refreshing drink after our walk. Two beer festivals are held at the Buck each year.

The Buck

There are two other pubs serving real ale in Reeth, the **4** **King's Arms** and the **5** **Black Bull**. If you're wondering why the sign of the Black Bull is upside down, it was in response to a dispute with the National Park authority, which objected to a previous landlord taking the rendering off the walls. The render was replaced, but the sign remains upside down as a protest.

From Reeth, return across the village green and round to the bridge you crossed earlier and follow the road around to the right. As you see a house before you, there's a small path signposted Grinton that goes to the right of it at **G** ⊕ SE042990. Follow this all the way until it comes out at the road just before the bridge. Turn right onto the road and into the warming, cosy pub that is the **2** **Bridge Inn** – a 'muddy boots welcome' sign stands outside, and some cycling paraphernalia also suggests its popularity among road and mountain bikers. This former coaching inn dates back to the 15th century. The main room has a log-burning stove and there are postcards and money notes from around the world above the bar. Down to the right is another room with a dartboard. There are also a couple of restaurant areas and the food is excellent. On my visit the ales included Jennings Cumberland and Sneck Lifter, Thwaites Wainwright and a guest. The Thursday night music evening is popular and there are five guest bedrooms too.

PUB INFORMATION

1 **BUCK HOTEL**
Reeth, DL11 6SW
01748 884210 • buckhotel.co.uk • ⊨
Opening hours: 11–midnight

2 **BRIDGE INN**
Grinton, DL11 6HH
01748 884224 • bridgeinn-grinton.co.uk • ⊨
Opening hours: 12–midnight; 12–11 Sun

Try also:

3 **RED LION**
Langthwaite, DL11 6RE
01748 884218 • langthwaite-redlion.co.uk
Opening hours: 11am–3pm, 7pm–11pm Mon–Sat; 10.30am–3pm, 7pm–11pm Sun

4 **KING'S ARMS**
Reeth, DL11 6SY
01748 884259 • thekingsarms.com • ⊨
Opening hours: 11–11; 11–midnight Fri & Sat

5 **BLACK BULL**
Reeth, DL11
01748 884213 • theblackbullreeth.co.uk • ⊨
Opening hours: 8.30–midnight; 8.30–2am Fri, Sat

Spaunton Moor

WALK
9

It's the classic North York Moors landscape: a brooding heather moorland, vast views over the hills carved mellow during the last ice age, with the regular squawk of grouse as the soundtrack. During the summer the vivid heather flowers to a spectacular bloom. This walk, one of the shorter featured in this book, is a little-trod circular walk out of Cropton. It's a combination of pleasant lanes, exposed moorland and a couple of lovely villages (and their pubs). The route can be shortened considerably by starting and finishing in Lastingham. Despite the relatively diminutive size of Spaunton Moor, reaching just 290 metres (951 feet), it is wildly exposed to the weather that can turn in minutes. Hypothermia is common on the moorland because of the lack of shelter. Navigation on the main paths is pretty straightforward – but definitely take a map and compass in case the cloud comes down. Take binoculars too; there's an abundance of wildlife.

▶ **Start/finish:** Cropton

▶ **Access:** Pickering is accessible by train. Cropton has few transport links.

▶ **Distance:** 8.7 miles (14km)

▶ **Ascent:** 1154ft (352m)

▶ **Duration:** 4-6 hours

▶ **Fitness:** 👟👟

▶ **Navigation:** 🧭🧭

▶ **OS map:** Explorer OL27 & OL26 *North York Moors - Eastern area* and *Western area* (or Landranger 100 *Malton & Pickering*)

▶ **Local attractions:** North York Moors Railway, Dalby Forest, Castle Howard

▷ **THE PUBS:** New Inn, Cropton; Blacksmith's Arms, Lastingham; Moors Inn, Appleton-le-Moors

Lastingham Millennium Stone

Blacksmith's Arms, Lastingham

Cropton to Spaunton Moor

Our walk starts, and finishes, at the New Inn in Cropton, a brilliant family-run pub with a growing brewery attached. Turn left out of the pub car park and walk along Cropton Lane to the green triangle. Follow the signs to Lastingham and walk round to the left and downhill. Along most of this stretch is a mud path on the left hand side, but on occasions you'll have to jump onto the road. Take care as there are a couple of blind corners. You'll pass a sign that signifies you are entering the North York Moors National Park.

The North York Moors National Park covers 554 square miles (1,430km2) of North Yorkshire and includes one of the largest areas of heather moorland in the United Kingdom. We're entering the southern side of the park, which stretches along the coast in the east (see Walk 10), to the A19 in the west and up towards Guisborough in the north.

Continue down the hill, along the path where possible, to the bridge over Cropton Beck at **A** 🕓 SE752895. Turn left again following the road sign towards Lastingham.

We're now following a quiet lane (no pavement) past Beckhouse Farm and round to the left over Seven Bridge. At Lower Askew follow the road around to the right for a couple of hundred metres and then continue north onto an even narrower lane at **B** 🕓 SE742900. Continue along this track north until the path splits at **C** 🕓 SE742907. Don't take the left fork here, but continue until you see another gate on your left. Here a clear, wide green path climbs through the heather and onto the moor itself.

Across Spaunton Moor

Spaunton Moor is crisscrossed with paths, bridleways and tracks – it's often not that easy to determine exactly which one you are on. A sign above Lastingham states you can 'walk over open, unrestricted moorland – not fields or woodland' and according to Natural England all of the moorland part of this walk is Open Access. Note that there is a restriction on dogs here except guide, hearing, or assistance dogs. All this is a way of saying that, as you'll see from the map, the bridleway meanders slightly off the shooter's track, but the track is by far the easier one to follow.

BLACKSMITH'S ARMS

KEY

🚶 Walk start/finish

- - - Walk route

Lastingham

To Appleton-le-Moors

The lane towards Spaunton Moor   **Looking back towards Cropton from Spaunton Moor**

With that in mind, trot north along the rocky wide path and watch as the glorious views to the east and south open up. Britain is home to around 70 per cent of the world's moorland, and the North York Moors National Park has the largest continuous area in England and Wales. Spaunton Moor has an alarming amount of grouse – and by alarming I mean when they suddenly panic and fly out of the heather squawking. The moor is also home to many other ground nesting birds such as golden plover, lapwing, curlew and merlin. Ring ouzels are also increasing in numbers thanks to careful land management by the owners.

Even in poor weather, the shooters' track should be easy to follow. The next tick feature is a pile of stones marked on the map as Abraham's Hut. This large cairn and Bronze Age burial ground is to the right of the track. From here we begin to curve to the west towards our midpoint of Ana Cross, a very tall stone cross. The map displays several paths here, but there is one clear track that continues directly to Ana Cross. About half way towards it you'll be able to see it if the mist is up. If you can't see it, set a bearing to the cross and be sure you roughly follow it. The track itself passes to the right of the cross, but the weather would have to be really bad to miss it.

Ana Cross

Open moorland at Spaunton

At around 3.6 metres (12 feet) high, Ana Cross at **D** ⊙ SE724938, also known as Ain Howe Cross, is one of the tallest crosses of more than 30 over this area of the moors and is one of more than 1,000 across the North York Moors in total. There has been a cross here for more than 1,000 years to mark a route between Farndale and Rosedale. The one you see here is a replacement dating back to the 19th century, but the original, parts of which can be seen in the crypt in St Mary's church in Lastingham, was probably twice the height. Like the packhorses and tradespeople who used a cross here for navigation for hundreds of years before us, we'll do the same and use it to guide us back down towards Lastingham along Lastingham Ridge.

Partridge

From Ana Cross, our route heads directly south down an ancient path. After about 500 metres, we meet a track and follow a wide, rocky and boggy path down to Spring Heads Turn at **E** ⊙ SE724925. Continue along the ridge track gently falling down into the village of Lastingham. You'll see a fingerpost showing a crossroads just before a gate that leads onto a road by Lastingham Grange Hotel. Also here is the Lastingham Millennium Stone, carved by local artist Jennifer Tetlow. The stone marks AD2000 and also AD654, when the village was founded after a monastery was built here by King Ethelwald of Deira (for his own burial).

Lastingham is a well-preserved little village, notable for its ancient church and one excellent pub. St Mary's church was built on the site of Ethelwald of Deira's monastery with parts of the crypt dating back to 1078. The crypt has some amazing relics, including the original Ana Cross and more ancient stones. To reach the 🍺 **Blacksmith's Arms**, walk down past Lastingham Grange Hotel and turn right towards the church. The pub is opposite St Mary's.

The Blacksmith's Arms is a hugely welcoming country pub, the sort that has been part of the fabric of its community for many years. A sign on the door reads: 'To those who cross the threshold of this door, a hearty welcome both to rich and poor. One favour only we would bid you grant, feel you're at home and ask for what you want.' Well, OK then. Inside the 18th-century pub, it's even more welcoming with an open fireplace and dozens of pewter mugs hanging from the ceiling. It's incredibly cosy as you sit among junkets collected from over the decades and the layout in the bar make it impossible not to fall into conversation with someone else.

Blacksmith's Arms (above and right)

One piece of gossip recounted on the pub's website is of the Rev Jeremiah Carter who was told off by his superiors for 'playing and dancing in the pub on the Sabbath'. His wife ran the pub in order to earn money to pay for their 13 children. His excuse, after persuading the parishioners to stay for a drink after the service, was to play the fiddle and encourage dancing to stop them from drinking so much. Apparently the Archdeacon believed it.

In all it's what a pub should be, made all the more remarkable by the fact that it can quietly seat lots of diners in adjacent rooms – the steak and ale pie comes highly recommended. On tap when I visited were Shepherd Neame Spitfire, Theakston Best, Black Sheep and Seraphim from Sonnet 43 Brew House in County Durham. There are also three guest rooms available.

PUB INFORMATION

 BLACKSMITH'S ARMS
Anserdale Lane, Lastingham, YO62 6TN
01751 417247 • blacksmithslastingham.co.uk • 🏠
Opening hours: 11.30-11.30

 NEW INN
Cropton Lane, Cropton, YO18 8HH
01751 417330 • newinncropton.co.uk • 🏠
Opening hours: 11-11 (midnight Fri & Sat)

Try also:

 MOORS INN
Appleton-le-Moors, YO62 6TF
01751 417435 • moorsinn.co.uk • 🏠
Opening hours: 11-11

Lastingham to Cropton

Now it's time for the pleasant jaunt back to Cropton. Leaving the pub, turn left out of the door and left again to retrace your steps back over the bridge crossing Ings Beck. At the end of the road, turn right on to High Street and then left on to Ings Lane. After about 100 metres look out for a fingerpost on the right just as the road curves slightly to the left. It is marked 'The Inn Way' and 'Public Footpath'. Follow this often-muddy path across a little stone bridge at **F** 🕐 **SE732903**, over a stile and through woodland.

The path emerges out on to open fields and leads along the fence against Hagg Wood. Eventually you'll see a gate that leads on to Birk Head Lane. Turn left onto this quiet road and into Lower Askew. Bear left through the buildings and then turn right back out on to the road that you'll recognise from earlier. From here, it is a matter of retracing your steps all the way back up to Cropton and directly to the **2 New Inn**.

The New Inn is a welcoming pub with a restaurant and accommodation and is home to the successful Great Yorkshire and Cropton Brewery. There's a huge choice of beers, including one made by Spandau Ballet's Tony Hadley and a range of three by the band Madness. There are few better ends to a walk than a pub like this.

Also worth visiting is the 17th-century **3 Moors Inn** in nearby Appleton-le-Moors, three miles from Cropton.

Whitby to Staithes

Whitby and the cove-hidden villages along the coastline of the North York Moors National Park are some of the country's most picturesque places. The wild North Sea batters the cliff edges, and sea defences stand proud protecting these tiny fishing settlements. It's a habitat for an incredibly diverse array of birdlife, yet this stretch of coastline is also replete with seafaring history, in particular that of Captain James Cook who lived in both Whitby and Staithes, the destination of our walk. We start in the wonderful town of Whitby, a place so loaded with history and intrigue it's worth spending a few days here. It also has some great pubs with several mentioned in the *Good Beer Guide*. This linear walk, which can be just as easily done backwards, leaves from the town's docks and follows the Cleveland Way north to Staithes, where there are regular buses back to Whitby and its pubs.

- **Start:** Whitby
- **Finish:** Staithes
- **Distance:** 11.5 miles (18.5km)
- **Access:** Regular Sapphire X4 buses between Staithes and Whitby
- **Ascent:** 1,978ft (603m)
- **Duration:** 5-7 hours
- **Fitness:**
- **Navigation:**
- **OS Maps:** Explorer OL27 *North York Moors – Eastern area*
- **Local attractions:** Whitby Abbey, Captain Cook Memorial Museum
- **THE PUBS:** Cod & Lobster; Captain Cook Inn, both Staithes; Little Angel Inn; Station Inn, both Whitby. Try also: Royal Hotel, Runswick Bay; Brown Cow, Hinderwell; Royal George, Staithes; Black Horse; Board Inn, both Whitby
- **Timing tip:** Be sure to leave time to get the bus back to Whitby. The bus stop is a good 10-minute walk from the Cod & Lobster in Staithes

Staithes harbour

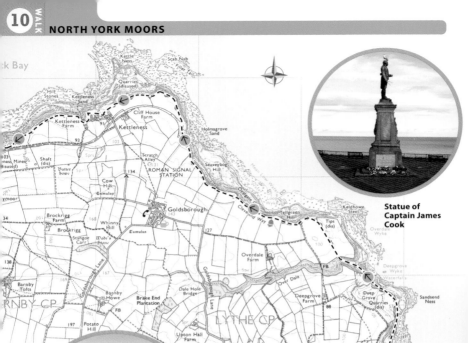

Statue of Captain James Cook

Whitby to Sandsend

This route begins on Bridge Street, at the western end of the bridge over the mouth of the River Esk. Built in 1908, this is a swing bridge that separates the upper and lower harbours, but there's been a bridge at this spot since around 1350. The seagoing vessels you'll see include commercial, fishing and pleasure cruisers. Lobsters, crab, cod and haddock are the mainstay catches; fish and chips on your return is a must. If you're setting off early in the morning you may pass some of the town's lively fish markets.

Walk north along the wonderfully named streets of St Ann's Staith, Haggersgate and Pier Road towards the pier. Both of the piers that guard the harbours are Grade II listed and each has a lighthouse. The Khyber Pass is next, which was named after the Afghan pass, although it's somewhat less dramatic. It was cut through the cliff under the stewardship of George Hudson, the 'Railway King' who brought the train to Whitby, opening it up for tourism. Take the path across the Pass (cutting off the corner), followed by the steps on the other side of the road opposite a car park. At the top you'll pass under the

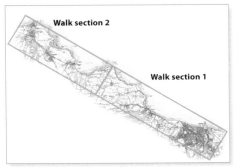

Walk section 2

Walk section 1

Right next to the whale bones is a bronze statue of this area's most famous son, Captain James Cook, erected in 1912. On this spot he has perhaps the best view of Whitby, the harbour and of course the famous 13th-century Gothic Abbey. James Cook moved from his birthplace in Marton to Staithes where we're heading, and then served his apprenticeship in Whitby. Four ships used by Cook on his voyages were built in Whitby, including the *Endeavour*.

famous Whale Bones Arch, huge jawbones from a whale. It's a reminder of the whaling tradition that was instrumental in Whitby's past fortunes. Between 1753 and 1833 there were 55 whaling ships operating out of the harbour, including one of the country's most successful, the *Jenny*. During this period more than 25,000 seals and 2,761 whales were brought back to Whitby. When the ships returned fully laden, they would display the whales' jawbones, inspiring this monument that was first put up in 1963. The whale bones you see here today replaced the original ones in 2002 and were donated by Anchorage in Alaska, a town that is twinned with Whitby. Don't forget the mandatory photo.

Just by the road near the statue is an acorn sign that will show our route throughout the walk and reflects that we'll be walking along a National Trail. In this case it's the Cleveland Way we're following, part of

Whitby

a 109-mile-long footpath that arches around the North York Moors National Park from Helmsley north to Saltburn-by-the-Sea and back down the coast through Whitby and Scarborough to finish in Filey.

We follow the acorn signs heading north. Beyond the green is the North Terrace, a place that was home to Bram Stoker the author of *Dracula*. Stoker stayed in a guesthouse here and drew inspiration from the town and views of the abbey, and indeed based some of the book in Whitby. It is said he even found the name 'Dracula' in the town's library while browsing local history. If you haven't read it, this trip is the perfect opportunity.

We continue along the top of the West Cliff above Whitby Sands towards Sandsend. The route stays on the cliff top until a steep descent at **A** 📍 **NZ881118**. Here the route turns inland, under a bridge and to the A174 to skirt around the Whitby Golf Club. There's a pavement along this unremarkable stretch of road all the way into Sandsend, and across the bridge at **B** 📍 **NZ862125**.

Sandsend to Kettleness

From the bridge, follow the curve of the road and walk along the pavement above the beach to the car park on your right just before the Wit's End Café. Walk through the stone archway into the car park. The Cleveland Way continues up a staircase at

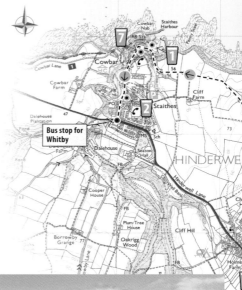

The picturesque town of Staithes

Looking back along the Cleveland Way

path to Kettleness. The views along this stretch, both north and south along the dramatic, sea-ravaged coastline, are spectacular. Yet it's what lies within the rock that some find most attractive. The cliffs along this route are so rich in fossils it's known as the Dinosaur Coast. The mudstone and limestone cliffs dating back to the Jurassic period, around 200 million years ago, are exposed all around the bays of the area. Ammonites are particularly common finds, and bones of Jurassic marine life are regularly found. Footprints from the Middle Jurassic period, a time when this area was delta, scrub and forest, as well as fossils from the Upper Jurassic period when the seas around here were tropical, are also regular finds among the cliffs between Staithes and Filey.

the far end. Head up the stairs, following the sign that reads 'Cleveland Way, Kettleness 3 Miles', and walk onto the wide path that looks as though it once was a railway line. Indeed, we soon see a disused tunnel along the route; we're going over the hill however. The trail heads up a series of steps, up and up, until it flattens out across wheat fields. Simply follow the clear

There's nothing tropical about the seas now however, this is a brisk section of coastline and its ever-changing look is testament to the raging North Sea. Keep

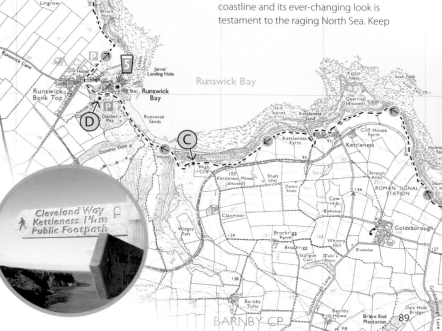

89

an eye on the National Trails website for any sections that may require a diversion because of a landslip. These are particularly evident along this stretch. The small settlement of Kettleness was itself moved back after a major landslip in 1829 that destroyed much of the village and the alum works. Alum works and quarries were a common sight around this area and much of the unnatural looking rock and landscape is likely to have been caused by them.

Kettleness to Port Mulgrave

From Kettleness, the trail twists slightly inland around a deep gorge and then heads back along the cliff edge. At **C** NZ817153 you'll notice a sign warning that occasional very high tides render the path that leads across the beach to Runswick Bay inaccessible. The sign advises you to wait until the tide recedes or follow the diversion offered (check www.tidetimes.org.uk/whitby-tide-times for details – note the address on the sign is incorrect and this is the correct one). We are now at what is perhaps the steepest section of the route. The footpath rapidly descends towards the west. It's largely steps, but take care especially when it's wet. Even on a dry day, it's going to be wet when you reach the bottom of Hob Holes – fortunately

Open farmland above Staithes

ENGLAND COAST PATH

As you walk the coastal section of the Cleveland Way, you'll notice signs on stiles and gates reading 'Part of the England Coast Path'. This ambitious project aims to create one of the world's longest coastal trails that will stretch 2,795 miles (4,500 kilometres) around England's coast linking up many existing paths and making the most of new Coast Access laws. The proposed completion date is in 2020.

there are handy wooden railings. From here, it's a walk along the beach to the idyllic village of Runswick Bay. This tiny village is home to a pleasantly ramshackle jumble of red-roofed buildings. Head towards them and walk up the stone ramp and onto the road that leads up to the left. The **5** **Royal Hotel** is a good spot for a pint of Black Sheep overlooking the beautiful bay. Walk up towards the main road, keeping an eye out for the Cleveland Way signs, and turn right at **D** NZ808159. The path zigzags sharply upwards past a bench blessed with fabulous views. At the top of the path follow the road to the Runswick Bay Hotel (that was being refurbished when I walked this route). Walk through the hotel car park and continue on the Cleveland Way, back along the coastal path and above the Lingrow Cliffs. The trail undulates through fields and to the junction at Port Mulgrave.

Lifeboat in Whitby harbour

Port Mulgrave to Staithes

Port Mulgrave was once a major ironstone-mining centre. Some of the industrial detritus remains below in the cove, including the pier that would have been used to transport the ore away – the full impressive wooden gantry is shown on an interpretation board. The mine eventually closed in the 1930s, succumbing to the lack of iron and the sea itself. The remaining structures were destroyed by the Royal Engineers at the beginning of World War II to prevent enemy landings.

Port Mulgrave is also the nearest access point to Hinderwell, a small village that is home to the 6 **Brown Cow**. It's about a 20-minute detour off our route, and also on the bus line back to Whitby.

From Port Mulgrave the fields open up offering fantastic views north to Boulby Cliffs, some of the highest cliffs in England, but you won't see much of Staithes from here, as it's hidden down in a cove. Several paths crisscross the fields, but at the gate, descend the abrupt hill along the cliff edge at the National Trust-managed Old Nab. The path skirts the cliffs, before rising slightly inland. Soon, the pleasing sight of Staithes comes into focus including the 7 **Cod & Lobster** precariously hanging on to the harbour. The route down is slightly more circuitous than it seems. Follow the trail inland around to the farm. The path is clearly signposted and heads down right behind the cottage. Another

signpost signals the direction into Staithes and down the High Street to the waterfront.

Staithes is a delightful village set between two cliffs and protected from the elements, mostly, by two harbour walls. At the turn of the 20th century, Staithes was one of the biggest fishing ports along this coast with some 80 boats heading out onto the choppy cold Atlantic. It was also an important source of alum, iron and potash. Today, a handful of fishermen remain in the village, as the boats attest, but you're just as likely to bump into one of the 'Staithes group' of artists these days. Readers with small children may also recognise the village as the filming location for the CBeebies television series *Old Jack's Boat* starring Bernard Cribbins.

Staithes is also home to several decent pubs. The Cod & Lobster has a winning location right on the harbour wall. On some occasions it has been a bit too close to the sea. In the great storm of 1953 the entire front of the pub was washed away. When the swell is high and a storm is in, it's advised to use the rear door lest you get a bit wet. Inside, however, this cosy and friendly pub offers a welcome haven from the wind and has a good seafood-heavy menu and excellent beer. On my visit, there was Theakston, Black Sheep, Timothy Taylor's Landlord and a delicious house beer brewed by North Yorkshire Brewing Company called Old Jack's Tipple, named after the CBeebies character. On a warm day enjoy your pint and fish and chips

Cod & Lobster   **Board Inn**

on the patio, in winter head to the fireside. Nearby is the **7** **Royal George** that also has real ales on tap.

The **2** **Captain Cook Inn** is handily on Staithes Lane, the road back out of the village towards the bus stop for Whitby. It has a wide range of guest ales on four or five handpumps, including the house beer, Northern Navigator, brewed by North York Brewing Company. It's also won the local CAMRA branch Pub of the Year award several times. It's the kind of place where dogs and muddy boots are welcome,

and therefore comes highly recommended.

From here, continue back along Staithes Lane to the A174 and just on the left is the bus stop. The Sapphire X4 leaves every half hour back to Whitby and takes 30 minutes.

Back in Whitby there is an abundance of pubs serving great beer, including the **8** **Black Horse**, **9** **Board Inn**, **3** **Little Angel Inn** and the **4** **Station Inn** where eight beers are available, plus good ciders. So plenty of places to enjoy a relaxing drink in after your long walk

PUB INFORMATION

1 **Cod & Lobster**
High Street, Staithes, TS13 5BH
01947 840330 • codandlobster.co.uk •
Opening hours: 10-11

2 **Captain Cook Inn**
60 Staithes Lane, Staithes, TS13 5AD
01947 840200 • captaincookinn.co.uk •
Opening hours: 11-midnight

3 **Little Angel Inn**
18 Flowergate, Whitby, YO21 3BA
01947 820475
Opening hours: 12-midnight (1am Fri & Sat)

4 **Station Inn**
New Quay Road, Whitby, YO21 1DH
01947 603937 • stationinnwhitby.co.uk •
Opening hours: 10-midnight; 10-11.30 Sun

Try also:

5 **Royal Hotel**
Runswick Bay, TS13 5HT
01947 840215 •
Opening hours: 12-5 Mon-Thu; 12-11 Fri-Sun

6 **Brown Cow**
55 High Street, Hinderwell, TS13 5ET
01947 840694 •
Opening hours: 11-midnight (1am Fri); 12-midnight Sun

7 **Royal George**
High Street, Staithes, TS13 5BH
01947 841432 • theroyalgeorgestaithes.co.uk •
Opening hours: 11.30-11.30 (12.30 Fri & Sat)

8 **Black Horse**
91 Church Street, Whitby, YO22 4BH
01947 602906 • the-black-horse.com •
Opening hours: 11-11; 12-10.30 Sun

9 **Board Inn**
125 Church Street, Whitby, YO22 4DE
01947 602884 • theboardinnwhitby.co.uk •
Opening hours: 11.30-11; 11-11 Sun

Scotland

Ben Nevis

It's the big one, the highest peak in Great Britain, the master of the Highlands, the Ben. The walk is challenging, beautiful, and slightly bizarre. There's no way we could leave the Ben out this book, not least of all when there's a handful of great pubs in the nearby town of Fort William, and one at the very base of the mountain itself. Despite the many thousands of walkers who climb, or attempt to climb, Ben Nevis every year (an estimated 100,000) and the relatively simple navigation, it must not be underestimated. Benign conditions at the bottom, or even half way up, can turn into a blizzard at the top at any time of year. Snow rarely leaves Ben Nevis, fog is present more than half of the year, and the annual average temperature at the top, in July, is 3°C. In short, be well-prepared all year round. Be so, however, and the rewards are great.

▸ **Start/finish:** The Ben Nevis Inn, Achintee

▸ **Access:** Short taxi ride to Ben Nevis Inn. Fort William widely accessible by bus and train.

▸ **Distance:** 9 miles (15km)

▸ **Ascent:** 4,301ft (1,311m)

▸ **Duration:** 6-9 hours

▸ **Fitness:**

▸ **Navigation:**

▸ **OS map:** Explorer 392 *Ben Nevis & Fort William*

▸ **Local attractions:** Ben Nevis Distillery, golf, Nevis Range mountain gondola, skiing in winter

▸ **THE PUBS:** Ben Nevis Inn, Achintee; Grog & Gruel, Cobbs at Nevisport, Great Glen, Fort William.

▸ **Timing tip:** It's almost impossible to predict the duration of this walk. It's long and hard so always leave as early as possible.

The seemingly endless steps up towards Halfway Lochan

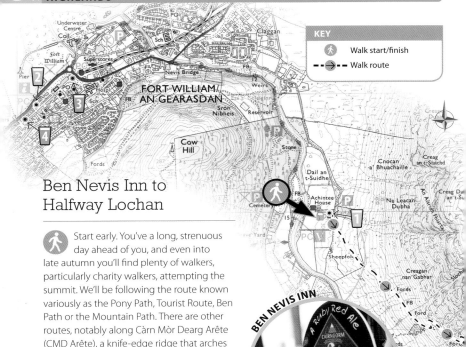

Ben Nevis Inn to Halfway Lochan

Start early. You've a long, strenuous day ahead of you, and even into late autumn you'll find plenty of walkers, particularly charity walkers, attempting the summit. We'll be following the route known variously as the Pony Path, Tourist Route, Ben Path or the Mountain Path. There are other routes, notably along Càrn Mòr Dearg Arête (CMD Arête), a knife-edge ridge that arches spectacularly to the summit, showing off the best of the precipitous north face. It's a route for very experienced hillwalkers and mountaineers only, and in very fine weather. It requires a head for heights and there's some scrambling. Given the prevailing weather conditions, we'll be taking the Mountain Path that is fairly straightforward until you reach the summit plateau. It's an up-and-down route along a rocky path.

Our route starts at a pub, of course. The Ben Nevis Inn is a couple of miles away from the town of Fort William in Achintee. If you're staying in the town, it's a short taxi ride. There is alternatively a bunkhouse at the inn.

From the pub at Achintee, take note of the hilarious weatherboard and walk through the gate into Glen Nevis that curves around the mighty mountain. This is a lovely section of the walk, rising up through open fields and onto a rocky path that skips over waterfalls and zigzags up through woodland – enjoy it, as much of the walk is above the tree line and more barren. It also offers fabulous views of the Mamores range of mountains surrounding

the Glen including Mullach nan Coirean, Sgurr a'Mhaim and the fantastic looking Stob Ban, all fine options for a day walk.

The first destination on this route is Lochan Meall an t-Suidhe known, somewhat optimistically, as Halfway Lochan: it's neither, in height nor time. The path here is easy to follow but extremely rocky and care is needed in the wet. Occasionally you may need to put a hand down, especially as it bends back north-east, but it's certainly not anywhere near scrambling. The main path upwards is clear, and at **A** ☼ NN144721 carves back on itself, before continuing north-east and up to the right of the Lochan. There are other paths here, but signs ask walkers not to use them – like on many popular British mountains, erosion is a problem. Feel free to tut at those walking that seemingly shorter route (it's not), and follow the wide path.

The tallest mountains have always been popular destinations. The first recorded ascent of Ben Nevis was in 1771 by James Robertson, a Scottish botanist (intrepid botanists often achieved first ascents). In 1818, John Keats followed, writing a short sonnet opening with the lines:

Read me a lesson, Muse, and speak it loud
Upon the top of Nevis, blind in mist!

I look into the chasms, and a shroud
Vapourous doth hide them, -- just so
much I wist

It's a sentiment, never more eloquently put, that most visitors will experience. A year later the naturalist William MacGillivray complained of 'fragments of earthen and glass ware, chicken bones, corks, and bits of paper' at the summit. Today, it is empty packets of Quavers and cans of Strongbow that people complain of. Take a quick break on arriving at the Lochan that sits in the col between Ben Nevis and Meall an t-Suidhe climbing up to the west.

Walkers on the rock path near the start

Halfway Lochan to the summit

From the Lochan, if you look to your right you'll see, weather permitting, the route that starts to traverse the mountain proper around a couple of impressive gullies. The rock here is barren and scree ridden. Ben Nevis is a shivering hulk that was once, 350 million years ago, a vast volcano. Ben Nevis is all that's left of the inner dome of the volcano that collapsed on itself. Look down, what you're walking on is a mixture of granite and basaltic lava. The mountain, like the rest of the Highlands, has since been further smoothed by glaciation.

Follow the wide path to the junction at **B** ⊛ **NN147724**. Here, turn right to take the path south and gently uphill around the western flank. The path that continues north leads around to the CMD Arête and to the climbers' routes up the formidable jumble of buttresses, gullies and towers that make the north face of the Ben a climbers' Nirvana… if that Nirvana is extremely exposed, freezing cold, trapped by fierce winds, wet rock and with a very, very long drop. Throughout

the winter, climbers from around the world test their mettle on the winter and ice routes, some of the toughest in the world, thanks, in large part, to the often-horrendous weather conditions.

The first part of the walk traversing the mountain is pleasant and not too steep, with truly wonderful views down towards Fort William and across the Highlands. Some deride Ben Nevis for its popularity and the relative dullness of the walk up and down, but perhaps they never stopped to look around. The views are the principal treat in climbing this mountain via the Mountain Path. At **C** ⊛ **NN146715**, the path begins its zigzag up towards the summit. It also begins to get rockier — you'll be thankful for some ankle support, and that chocolate bar. It is tough going here, particularly near the top when the route becomes more indistinct. As the path flattens out, begin to layer up and take note of your compass. As mentioned before, the weather up here is often foul and with very low visibility. It's also likely to be significantly windier than the relatively sheltered western flank. The etymology of Ben Nevis can be traced back and translated to 'the mountain with its

The view south-west from above Halfway Lochan

head in the clouds'. An alternative is 'venomous mountain'. Either are fairly accurate descriptions.

Looking into Glen Nevis

The top of Ben Nevis is an indistinct, rocky plateau roughly in the shape of a crescent moon. An Ordnance Survey trig point, a tall shelter and the remains of an observatory are all located on the eastern end of the summit. To the north is a steep drop. The path is reasonably clear and marked by cairns, although don't rely on these alone – be sure to take a couple of compass bearings. The path passes closely to the northern gullies, including Gardyloo that descends into the abyss, be sure to dogleg around these. In snow, when the path is hidden, it would be essential to take a couple of very accurate compass bearings. Severe cornices are also common.

Eventually, you'll come across what seems like an ancient Incan ruin. These are the remains of a meteorological observatory built in the 1870s by the Scottish Meteorological Society. Ponder the dedication of one Clement Lindley Wragge (known as Inclement Rag) who traipsed up to the summit every day during one summer to take readings. Between 1883 and 1904, the Ben Nevis Observatory was continuously manned. One of the scientists, Charles Thomson Rees Wilson, invented the cloud chamber used to detect ionising radiation, based on his observations of clouds during a couple of weeks he spent at the observatory. He won the Nobel Prize in physics for his discoveries.

Also on the summit is a trig point on top of a large cairn. Stand here and you are, briefly, the highest person in Britain at 1,344 metres (4,411ft) and, in fact, the highest for more than 400 miles until you reach the mountains of Norway. Well, almost. For that to truly happen, you need to climb to the emergency summit shelter that is a couple of metres higher than the trig point.

Summit to the Ben Nevis Inn

From the summit trig point at **D** 🔍 **NN166712**, it is time to retrace your steps all the way back down to the pub, but first you need to navigate off the mountain. This is probably the trickiest part of navigation on this walk if you're in the cloud, to ensure you're returning the same way, along the path heading west as marked on the OS maps. Be careful here not to descend to the south, but west back on the mountain path. Two bearings are required to dogleg around Gardyloo to the north and Five Finger Gully that lies below to the south-west. If you recognise the way you came up you should be fine. This isn't a route description designed for snow, but extra care is needed even if there's a dusting. From here, it's a long slog back down and, if you've set off early, dozens of people will be asking the same question: 'how far do you reckon mate?'.

Like all of the highest mountains worldwide, Ben Nevis holds some mythology. A commonly recounted tale is that the Ben is the mountain throne of Beira or Cailleach Bheur, a mythological figure who is considered the mother of all the gods and goddesses in Scottish mythology. From her throne she turned her negligent maid Nessa into, yes, Loch Ness and built the mountains around her from a magic hammer. She is also the personification of winter. And that's part

Ben Nevis Inn   **Grog & Gruel**

of the popularity of Ben Nevis. It's the highest mountain in the British Isles, but there's also a magnetic grasp on such a vast, intricate mountain that lies beyond mere statistics. It may not be the most thrilling ascent, but each step reveals something new.

Something to ponder as you enjoy a pint in the **Ben Nevis Inn** – a warm and cosy pub that handily sits right at the end of the trail. It's converted from farm buildings, but has a homely feel more reminiscent of an alpine lodge than a pub, with a log-burning fire, a mezzanine with Chesterfield sofas, and climbing paraphernalia scattered artfully

around the place. The long tables inspire a convivial atmosphere. The beer is also better than in most Alpine huts. On my visit there were beers from local-ish breweries Cairngorm, Isle of Skye and the very small An Teallach Ale Company. There's not a more welcoming place for a beer after a long day on the mountain. There's also a basic bunkhouse here, useful for an early start.

In Fort William itself, the pick is the **Grog & Gruel**, run by the same people as the fantastic Clachaig Inn. It's the place for outdoor enthusiasts, of whom there's always plenty in this town being so close to Ben Nevis, at the end of the West Highland Way and surrounded by some of the best mountains in the Highlands.

The pub is a fairly loud and fun place to go for a beer and some good food. There are six ever-changing pumps of often local real ales, and more good lagers on keg. On my visit, beers from the fantastic Williams Bros dominated. Beer festivals are held at the Grog & Gruel and it is regularly recognised by the local CAMRA branch. There's also a good whisky selection.

Also regularly recommended in the *Good Beer Guide* is **Cobbs** at Nevisport, a pleasant bar within an outdoor centre. There's a large fire, mountaineering photos on the wall and four handpumps with a changing selection of beer. Another recommendation is a newly built Weatherspoons pub under a Travelodge, the **Great Glen**. It has ten handpumps with many Scottish beers.

PUB INFORMATION

BEN NEVIS INN
Achintee Road, Claggan, PH33 6TE
01397 701227 • ben-nevis-inn.co.uk •
Opening hours: 12-11 (limited hours and days in winter)

GROG & GRUEL
66 High Street, Fort William, PH33 6AE
01397 705078 • grogandgruel.co.uk
Opening hours: 12-11.30 (12.30am Thu-Sat); 12.30 (5 in winter)-11.30 Sun.

Try also:

COBBS AT NEVISPORT
Airds Crossing, Fort William, PH33 6EU
01397 704790 • cobbs-at-nevisport.co.uk
Opening hours: 11-midnight (1am Fri & Sat);
12.30-midnight Sun

GREAT GLEN
104 High Street, Fort William, PH33 6AD
01397 709910
Opening hours: 7-midnight (1am Fri & Sat)

Glen Coe and Buachaille Etive Mòr

Across the vast moorland plains of Rannoch Moor, a pleasingly pyramidal mountain guards the entrance to Glen Coe: the great bulk of Buachaille Etive Mòr. It's one of the most photographed of all Scotland's mountains for a few reasons – its shape, its location welcoming visitors to the Highlands, the panoramic views from its summits and its majestic beauty. Popular among Munro-baggers and shown to the world in James Bond's *Skyfall*, Buachaille Etive Mòr provides one of the finest high mountain walks in the area. It would also be impossible to write a book like this without the inclusion of the Clachaig Inn, probably the most important pub in Scotland for mountaineering history.

▶ **Start/finish:** Altnafeadh car park

▶ **Access:** This is the least accessible walk by public transport in the book. Buses between Glasgow and Fort William stop at Kings House some three miles away. Buses also stop in Glencoe Village.

▶ **Distance:** 8 miles (13km)

▶ **Ascent:** 3,854ft (1,175m)

▶ **Duration:** 4.5-6.5 hours

▶ **Fitness:**

▶ **Navigation:** 😈 😈 😈

▶ **OS map:** Explorer 384 *Glen Coe & Glen Etive*

▶ **Key attractions:** Clachaig Inn, Loch Linnhe

▶ **THE PUBS:** Clachaig Inn, Glencoe Inn

▶ **Timing tip:** Night seems to descend very quickly, so start early. Check River Coupall is crossable.

Our route weaves up behind Stob Dearg on the left

Walking towards the Scottish Mountaineering Council's Lagangarbh Hut

Among the little-populated Highlands, it's often difficult to walk out of a pub or village and straight up a mountain. Buachaille Etive Mòr is a short drive east along the busy Pass of Glencoe from the Clachaig Inn. There are two places to park nearby, both often busy in summer. For this walk, the best place to park is at Altnafeadh, although the walk finishes at the other car park just under a kilometre west along the A82, so that's also an option.

Buachaille Etive Mòr is an exposed mountain surrounded by rivers on all sides. Along its five-mile ridge are four main tops. At the north-east end is the highest of the summits, Stob Dearg at 1,022 metres. Following the ridge south-west, it then crosses Stob na Doire (1,011 metres), Stob Coire Altrium (941 metres) and then finally reaches the magnificent outpost of Stob na Bròige at an impressive 956 metres. As further incentive to walk the whole thing, the first summit Stob Dearg and the last Stob na Bròige are Munros, the latter only being deemed so by the Scottish Mountaineering Council in 1997.

Our walk ascends steeply up to the col above Coire na Tulaich before rising up to Stob Dearg. We then briefly retrace our steps before following the curving ridge all the way along to Stob na Bròige. From the final summit we retrace our path for about a kilometre before descending down into Lairig Gartain for the long walk out. Although there are no scrambles, there are two places

Clachaig Inn

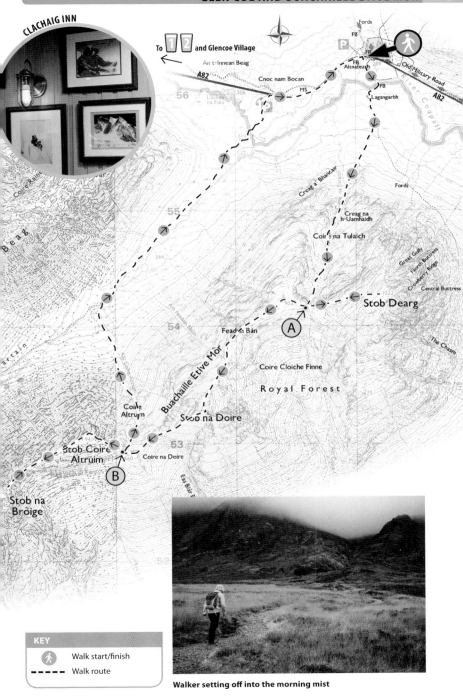

CLACHAIG INN

To 1 2 and Glencoe Village

An t-Innean Beag

A82

Cnoc nam Bocan

MS

Lochan
na Fola

Fords

FB

Altnafeadh

FB

Old Military Road

A82

River Coupall

Lagangarbh

FB

Fords

Creag a' Bhancair

Creag na
h-Uamhaidh

Coire na Tulaich

Great Gully

North Buttress

Crowberry Ridge

Central Buttress

Stob Dearg

Coire Ràm

Beag

Fead an Bàn

(A)

Coire Cloiche Finne

Royal Forest

The Chasm

Buachaille Etive Mòr

Coille
Altruim

Stob na Doire

Stob Coire
Altruim

Coire na Doire

(B)

Eas Bàr Fèith

Stob na
Bròige

KEY

Walk start/finish

Walk route

Walker setting off into the morning mist

at least, one on the ascent and one on the descent where the route is steep and you'll need to put your hand down. You may also need to slide on your bottom. As ever, the weather in the Highlands can change in seconds, so make sure you are fully equipped. In short, this is a fairly straightforward walk, but one for experienced hillwalkers. In winter this is a full-on mountaineering expedition requiring the use of ice axe and crampons. There are also serious avalanche dangers on the ascent and descent routes and there have been several fatalities. This route presumes there's no snow on the ground.

From the car park, you'll see the whitewashed Lagangarbh Hut owned by the Scottish Mountaineering Council (SMC). It was originally a crofting home. Bed space can be booked through the SMC's website but unlike a bothy, it remains locked. To get there descend to the footbridge, cross the River Coupall and head past a sign for the area's principal landowner, the National Trust for Scotland. Take a moment at the

Buachaille Etive Mòr

Lagangarbh Hut – some of the world's best mountaineers have stayed here (and indeed in the more comfortable surroundings of the Clachaig Inn). Sir Chris Bonington, Doug Scott and the late Dougal Haston all frequented this hut. Writing in the *Alpine Journal* after Haston's death in an avalanche in 1977, Scottish mountaineer Jimmy Marshall recalls: 'Dougal and Ronnie [Marshall] followed up a Lagangarbh work-party, to cover their newly painted 'lavatory green' walls with brilliant mind-blowing murals, reminiscent of Kandinsky; ostensibly in a vain attempt to counter the external Glencoe gloom!'

Gloom or no gloom, the walk up Coire na Tulaich is steep and energy sapping but largely straightforward. Just after the hut, the path splits. The left hand fork goes around to the head of Stob Dearg for a climbing approach, but we're following the right hand fork into the jaws of the coire. Creag a'Bhancair rises forebodingly above you to the right and Creag na h-Uamhaidh is to the left. The rocky path to the col is well

The first ascent lies behind Lagangarbh Hut

trodden and maintained – it'll be the longest staircase you've ever climbed. There are parts, especially when it crosses the streambed, when the path is lost among a jumble of rocks, but generally stay to the right of the stream and you'll find the clear path again. As you rise, it gets steeper, with only the occasional need for a steadying hand.

As you near the col, the path crosses some unpleasant scree. (When is scree ever pleasant?) Here the path is at its most indistinct and steepest; again you may need to put a hand down. The col is reached at around **A** ⊗ NN216541. Once you're on it you'll know; it's a broad saddle. On my last visit I heard the unmistakable crack of the ptarmigan at this point. From the col, there are around 140 metres of ascent to the summit of Stob Dearg, but nothing is as steep as the section you've just come up and it all seems a bit of a relief. The path, as on most of the walk, is fairly clear. Be sure to stay on the highpoint up the ridge and you can't go far wrong. Resist the temptation to descend on other paths that lead to climber's gullies.

MUNROS

Any chat about hillwalking in Scotland inevitably comes around to the subject of 'Munros'. To the uninitiated, Munros are Scottish mountains over 3,000 feet high. There are 282 Munros and some hillwalkers spend a lifetime 'bagging' all of them.

It's not quite as simple as all that of course. The status of a Munro depends on its topographical prominence. A Munro top is a mountain that while still over 3,000 feet, isn't regarded as a separate mountain.

It was mountaineer Sir Hugh Munro, a founding member of the Scottish Mountaineering Club, who first produced the *Munro's Tables* in 1891.

Mountains aren't, of course, uniform and measuring these mountains, and the prominence, is always cause for debate. Occasionally, the recorded height of a Munro changes because of improvements in technology and this is the cause of much consternation among the Munro-baggers as another mountain is now considered a Munro, or worse, one is demoted. For example, in 2009, Sgùrr nan Ceannaichean, was found to be four feet short of the magic number. And it is this arbitrary height that can annoy some people. Sgùrr nan Ceannaichean may get a lot less traffic as a result of its demotion to a mere Corbett (yes, that's a mountain in Scotland between 2,500 to 3,000 feet). We could go on… A Graham is between 2,000 and 2,500 feet and with a prominence of at least 500 feet. And if lists are your thing, then there are plenty more. Deep breath: in Scotland there are also Murdos and Donalds, and in England and Wales there are Furths, Hewitts, Nuttals, Wainwrights, Birketts, Simms, Deweys, Hardys, Humps, Marilyns and County Tops. So whether you enjoy ticking lists off or not, they do remain a great way to structure your hillwalking.

The unmistakable Buachaille Etive Mòr

Crossing River Coupall

There are a couple of false summits before the ridge narrows slightly and the final summit shelter cairn at 1,022 metres is reached. This is the highest point of the day. If it's clear the views here are huge, especially across the relentless bleakness of Rannoch Moor: 50 square miles of boggy moorland. Below you are famous climbing gullies and buttresses. One, Crowberry Ridge, was first climbed in 1900 by the Abraham Brothers – a famous climbing and photography duo (see Walk 5 for more about them). The Grade 3 scrambling route up the Curved Ridge is also below you.

Retrace your steps back to the col you ascended to above Coire na Tulaich. From here, the path leads clearly along, ascending to the left of a couple of small lochans before arching back to the left. There's a small descent here, before the surprisingly sheer looking ascent to the summit of Stob na Doire. Take care in mist not to descend below the col at 893 metres. Intimidating as it looks, the path up the ridge is actually very straightforward to follow, but steep in places. It's a slog, but there's a reward at the top.

Clachaig Inn in winter

From the summit cairn at 1,011 metres there are unbelievable views across the western summits up towards Ben Nevis. Buachaille Etive Beag is the parallel mountain ridge. To the south-east is the drama of the intricately carved Clach Leathad and the brooding mountains beyond. To the west, the Three Sisters of Glen Coe on Bidean nam Bian can be clearly seen – three steep ridges that descend dramatically towards the road – and Loch Leven glimpsed beyond that. You'll also see (if it's clear) the rest of the ridge walk along to Stob na Bròige.

Firstly, however, you need to negotiate the surprisingly steep descent down to the saddle above Coire Altruim. The path is clear, but care is needed especially in the wet. From the col, our route rises again to the 860-metre mark. Just over this point is the path that we'll be descending on later. Take note and prepare yourself for the last major climb of the day to the summit of Stob Coire Altruim. Again the views from the top make this ascent worthwhile. There's a cairn at the top. From here, the final ridge below Stob na Bròige can look worryingly narrow, but once you're actually on it, there'll be few problems – although take care in extremely high winds. Before you know it, you'll be at the summit shelter cairn on Stob na Bròige admiring the glorious views to the west.

Retrace your steps back across the ridge and Stob Coire Altruim (there's a path that cuts across below the summit here), and down to the path at **B** ⊗ NN200529. Although the descent down into Lairig Gartain is quick, it's probably the least pleasant part of the day – walking poles would be an advantage on this knee-crushing decline. As the path merges with the stream it's very steep in places. Pick your way very carefully through the ankle-eating rocks. In some places it may require an ungraceful bottom-slide or careful climb down.

Not quite quickly enough, the path flattens out down towards the River Coupall cutting through the fabulous Lairig Gartain, which translates rather literally as, the Valley of the Ticks. In summer, the midges are, well, noticeable! This swooping valley is almost

inconceivably vast. During late September to early November, it is one of the best places in the country to see the annual stag rutting. The roars from the red deer stags echo around this valley at an alarmingly loud volume. Yet, only when you make out the red deer – present, but quieter at other times of the year – do you get perspective on the size of this valley.

The red deer is the largest land mammal in the UK and stags can stand as high as 137 centimetres at the shoulder and weigh up to 190 kilograms. These animals, native to Britain, are most impressive and if nothing else, will take your mind off the slog back to the road. Hop across the stepping stones that cross River Coupall, be wary if it's up high, and follow the clear path back to the A82. It's a good couple of kilometres along here to the road and to what is probably the most dangerous part of the walk – the stretch back to the car at the Altnafeadh car park. There is a path to the right of the road barrier for some of it. It's a very, very dangerous road and I do not recommend walking along it.

The ascent to Stob na Doire

Clachaig Inn (above and right)

Now it's a short drive back to the **Clachaig Inn** for some great ales, good food and probably a wee dram. Like the Wasdale Head Inn in the Lake District (see Walk 5), the Clachaig Inn has cemented its place in British mountaineering history. Just a glance around the walls informs you of this inn's importance. Here we have signed pictures from some of the world's greatest mountaineers: Doug Scott and Alan Hinkes, who writes the foreword in this book, are present. In one picture taken at the seventh Scottish Mountaineering Council meeting held at the inn at Easter 1906, we see William W Naismith who worked out the formula, known as Naismith's rule, for walking speeds on mountains. There's J Norman Collie who pioneered climbs in the Cuillin Ridge in the Isle of Skye and later climbed in the Alps and Himalaya, and also Sir Hugh Munro who gave his name to the Munros we've just climbed. It was also in this inn that Hamish MacInnes founded the Glencoe Mountain Rescue Team in 1962. On the wall are some of the first ice axes made by MacInnes himself that changed the way ice axes were made.

A sign on the door reads 'No Hawkers or Campbells' in reference to the Massacre of Glencoe, a harrowing incident in 1692, when the 38 members of the Clan MacDonald of Glencoe were murdered by people who they had extended hospitality to after the Jacobite uprisings. Some of the women and children escaped but 40 later died from exposure after their homesteads were burned. Some of those under the command of Captain Robert Campbell of Glenlyon were also Campbells. A memorial now stands in the village of Glencoe.

Aside from all the history, the Clachaig Inn is also worthy of a regular entry in the *Good Beer Guide* thanks to a wide range of cask ales, mostly from Scottish breweries including Strathaven, Cairngorm and Williams Bros, served across the 15 handpumps on three bars. There is also a range of 300 malts – perfect after a day on the mountains.

Also worth trying is the **Glencoe Inn** in Glencoe Village. It's an upmarket hotel, but there's a pleasant bar with a couple of handpumps.

PUB INFORMATION

Clachaig Inn
Glencoe, Argyll, PH49 4HX
01855 811252 • clachaig.com •
Opening hours: 11-11

Glencoe Inn
Glencoe Village, Argyll, PH49 4HP
01855 811245 • crerarhotels.com •
Opening hours: 11-11

Winter alfresco dining at the Clachaig Inn

Ben Vrackie from Pitlochry

By the delightful town of Pitlochry and the even more picturesque outlying village of Moulin is the hulking great mountain of Ben Vrackie. Unlike many of the rounded peaks of the Cairngorms, the 841-metre Ben Vrackie is pleasingly pointy, almost Alpine in appearance. Our walk starts out a little outside of Pitlochry and ascends gently through woodland before emerging onto exposed moor dotted with lochans. Yet dominating almost the entire walk is Ben Vrackie, its summit indicator clearly visible from the start of the route. Disconcerting is the fact you seem to arrive almost directly underneath the vast, cliff-like southern face before the sharp 300-metre pull to the top. It's hugely rewarding, however, climbing up to the summit with outstanding views all around. Back down in Moulin and Pitlochry there are three excellent pubs, including the cosy and inviting Moulin Inn that also has its own brewery. Navigationally, it is quite straightforward, but the weather can turn in an instant.

▶ **Start/finish:** Craigvrack Hotel, Pitlochry

▶ **Access:** Frequent trains and buses serve Pitlochry

▶ **Distance:** 7.5 miles (12km)

▶ **Ascent:** 2,572ft (784m)

▶ **Duration:** 4-6 hours

▶ **Fitness:**

▶ **Navigation:**

▶ **OS map:** Explorer OL49 *Pitlochry & Loch Tummel*

▶ **Local attractions:** Edradour Distillery, Pitlochry Festival Theatre, fishing

▶ **THE PUBS:** Craigvrack Hotel and Old Mill Inn, Pitlochry; Moulin Inn, Moulin

▶ **Timing tip:** Despite the relatively short distance, take into account a very steep ascent and descent.

Looking over Loch a' Choire from the slopes of Ben Vrackie

Pitlochry to Ben Vrackie summit

We start our walk at the Craigvrack Hotel. There are plenty of places to park on the streets close by. From in front of the hotel turn right and walk uphill towards Moulin. Pass over the mini roundabout, and head up to the Moulin Inn where we'll be returning to in a few hours. Turn left around the pub, noting the brewery on the right (open Monday to Friday 9-4.30 'Just come in and speak to the brewer'). Walk along Baledmund Road heading round to the north and follow the signs to 'Bealach Path & Ben-y-Vrackie', a commonly used alternative name. Ben Vrackie is also called Beinn Bhracaigh and the name itself means 'speckled mountain'. You should be able to see your destination already.

Walk along the road up to the official car park (park up here if you want to cut out a bit of walking) and head towards Moulin Burn, a stream that we'll follow for the first part of the walk. The burn has provided Moulin, which once had a bigger population than Pitlochry, with power for various industries including lint, tweed and saw mills. Back down in Pitlochry one of our pub stops, the Old Mill Inn, still has a working water mill powered by this burn.

A sign at the back of the car park reads 'Bealach Path & Ben-y-Vrackie 2½'. The uphill section now begins in earnest. You'll walk above the burn to the left and through some kissing gates. As the dirt road forks, follow the small round signs to the right. A small wooden footbridge crosses a stream and then you'll come out onto open moorland with Ben Vrackie still ahead but seemingly no closer.

The wide path weaves through the moorland that is spectacular during the summer heather bloom. The area today is used for sheep farming and grouse shooting. There's only one wide footpath and it's hard to go wrong. At **A** ⊗ **NN942613**, the path splits and is clearly signposted; we're following the 'Path to Ben-y-Vrackie'. Looking back to the south, Pitlochry and the valley formed by the River Tummel opens out with the lower hills beyond it. The River Tummel that starts its journey some 50 miles away at Loch Rannoch falls into the Tay just beyond Pitlochry.

Soon you'll reach a gate. Go through it and follow the path north to skirt around Meall na h-Aodainn Mòire and Stac an Fheidh. The track descends slightly around the rocky outcrop before Loch a' Choire and the dauntingly steep track up the right flank of Ben Vrackie come into focus. There's a small path leading around to the left of the loch,

Morning mist over Pitlochry

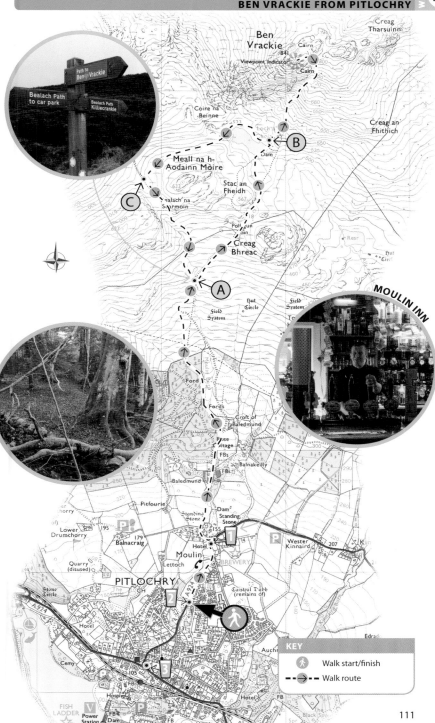

Ben
Vrackie
841

Creag
Tharsuinn

Cairn

Viewpoint Indicator

Cairn

Creag an
Fhithich

Coire na
Beinne

Lochan

B

Dam

Meall na h-
Aodainn Mòire

C

Bealach na
Sgairmoin

Stac an
Fheidh
567

Poll'gun
oin

Creag
Bhreac

A

Hut
Circle

Field
System

Resr

Hut
Circle

Field
System

Ford

Ford

Croft of
Baledmund

se
Cottage
FBs

FBs

Balnakeilly

Baledmund

MOULIN INN

Pitfourie

Standing
Stone

Dam
Standing
Stone

Lower
Drumchorry
195

179
Balnacraig

Hotel

155

Wester
Kinnaird
207

Moulin

Lettoch

BREWERY

Quarry
(disused)

PITLOCHRY

A924

Caisteal Dubh
(remains of)

Stone
Circle

A921

Hotel

Cemy

Hotel

Edra

FISH
LADDER

Power
Station

Dam

Port-na-
Craig

Hotel

82

Explorers'
Garden

Black Spo

111

Walk start/finish

Walk route

but we're heading directly across the arrow-straight dam to the right of the loch with a bench at the end. At the bench, take a deep breath and begin the long slog up.

Much of the path is like a rocky staircase, and there's no option other than to grin and bear it. It is slippery in parts, especially when there's ice on the ground. Don't forget to keep looking around, the views just get better and better. You're unlikely to go wrong here, just keep climbing. Some parts are steeper than others, particularly so as you near the top, but it's never exposed.

The well-maintained path takes you right up to the summit indicator, dedicated to the memory of John Brian Gray who died in the Household Cavalry in 1947. On top of the indicator, the direction of all the mountains is marked around a bronze plate. Most striking is the range around Beinn a' Ghlò to the north, just over the border of the Cairngorms National Park. Also clear (on a good day at least) is Schiehallion to the west – another great destination for a walk.

At 2,757 feet, Ben Vrackie falls 243 feet short of the magic Munro status of 3,000 feet. It is,

Walkers descending Ben Vrackie towards Loch a' Choire

Woodland near the end of the walk

however, eligible for the Corbett category. Climber John Rooke Corbett compiled the list of Corbetts in the 1920s. These are mountains that are between 2,500 and 3,000 feet (762 to 914m) in height, with a prominence of at least 500 feet. There are 222 Corbetts in all and there are 282 Munros. The trig point sits just below the viewpoint indicator.

It's also worth taking the time to explore the eastern summits. A gently undulating, wide ridge heads to a top marked on the map as Creag Tharsuinn.

Ben Vrackie summit to Pitlochry

Return to the viewpoint indicator and descend again east and then south along the path you came up, taking care all the way down as it's often slippery. Back just above the dam at Loch a' Choire at **B** NN948625, you can either return the way you came or turn right on the path that skirts around the loch. This route describes the latter. Follow the narrower path with the loch down below you to the left and head around the far end of the loch and past the protruding rock island.

The path continues west, ascending slightly around Meall na h-Aodainn Mòire

before descending again to the wider track at **C** NN938622. Turn left at this point. The path climbs through Bealach na Searmoin before meeting again the path we came up on at **A** NN942613. Follow the fingerpost marked 'Bealach Path to car park', going back over the footbridge and through the woodland to the car park. Then return the way you came up back into the village of Moulin and to the **Moulin Inn**.

The Moulin Inn, part of the Moulin Hotel, is a *Good Beer Guide* regular and one of the most delightful pubs in the area, offering a warm welcome, a cosy bar and a log fire. In the summer, the beer garden is popular with walkers and good food is on offer all year round.

The Moulin Inn has been welcoming weary walkers since 1695. According to the comprehensive history on the hotel's website, the original inn was much smaller with two rooms downstairs and two upstairs. Local elders used one of the rooms to arbitrate disagreements. Apparently, they could also sentence against minor misdemeanours by tying the wrongdoer to a tree to become a target for rotten fruit.

The bar serves its own beers from the Moulin Brewery that sits behind the pub in the former coach house and stables. If the brewery is open just poke your nose through

113

Moulin Inn

Old Mill Inn

the door and say hello. It first opened in 1995, and still mostly sells out of the pub, but bottles can be bought to take away. The ruby Ale of Atholl is their flagship beer and brewed in the Scottish 80/- style.

Moulin was once the largest village in the area, but Pitlochry began its expansion in the late 1700s as General Wade constructed a new road along the Tummel and Tay. However, it was during Victorian times when Pitlochry really grew. The Queen visited in 1842, the railway arrived in 1863 and Pitlochry's destination as a pleasant tourist-focussed town on the edge of the Cairngorms was cemented.

PUB INFORMATION

Moulin Inn
11-13 Kirkmichael Road, Moulin, PH16 5EH
01796 472196 • moulininn.co.uk •
Opening hours: 11-11

Craigvrack Hotel
38 West Moulin Road, Pitlochry, PH16 5EQ
01796 472399 • craigvrack.com •
Opening hours: 11-11

Old Mill Inn
Mill Lane, Pitlochry, PH16 5BH
01796 474020 • theoldmillpitlochry.co.uk •
Opening hours: 11-11; 11-midnight Sat & Sun.

From the Moulin Inn, walk back towards Pitlochry and the ☐ **Craigvrack Hotel**. The Craigvrack is a family run hotel with a good bar that has two changing guest beers on tap. Regulars have a say in which beers appear next.

Walking or driving towards Pitlochry, just continue downhill along West Moulin Road until you reach the centre of the village. Turn left onto Atholl Road and then left again into a pedestrianised road to reach our final pub recommendation, the ☐ **Old Mill Inn**. It is a popular place built within a 19th-century mill. A mill wheel still turns outside. Inside there are usually four or five beers on handpump, plus some interesting and local kegged beer. Excellent ales from nearby StrathBraan Brewery is always on.

While in this part of the world, it would also be rude not to mention two fabulous distilleries in the town. Blair Athol Distillery is located just to the east of the town out along the main road. It's open daily between 10 and 4, with more limited hours during the winter. The highly recommended Edradour Distillery, a favourite in these parts, is about a mile outside of Pitlochry and describes itself as the 'smallest distillery in Scotland'. It's open 9.30-5 Monday to Saturday and 12-5 on Sunday but closed in the middle of winter. Pick up a bottle as a souvenir of this lovely day out.

Cairn Gorm and the Northern Corries

The mighty Cairngorm plateau has been riven and beaten over millions of years by unimaginable geological forces to become Britain's only arctic terrain. But it has never been tempered. The Cairngorms are wild. On this walk we climb deep into the Cairngorm massif to the peak of the mountain that gives the range, and the national park, its name: Cairn Gorm. Up on these mountains, the highest, coldest and windiest in the UK, are five of Scotland's six highest peaks, and some amazing wildlife, including mountain hare, ptarmigan, snow bunting and golden eagles.

▶ **Start/Finish:** CairnGorm Mountain ski centre car park

▶ **Access:** Bus from Aviemore (number 31)

▶ **Distance:** 6 miles (10km)

▶ **Ascent:** 2,631ft (802m)

▶ **Duration:** 4-6 hours

▶ **Fitness:** ▲▲▲

▶ **Navigation:** ✪✪✪✪

▶ **OS Map:** Explorer OL57 *Cairn Gorm & Aviemore*

▶ **THE PUBS:** Glenmore Lodge; Old Bridge Inn, Cairngorm Hotel, Winking Owl, Aviemore

▶ **Local attractions:** CairnGorm Mountain ski resort, Glenmore Lodge courses, Strathspey Steam Railway, Cairngorm Reindeer Centre

▶ **Timing tip:** Be sure to check the times for the bus back to Aviemore.

Crossing Allt Coire an t-Sneachda

Looking back over the Queen's Forest

Our walk starts at the Cairn Gorm Mountain ski centre, about 10 miles (16km) out of Aviemore, and soon gets wild, rising above Coire an Lochain and over Stob Coire an t-Sneachda, before the final pull up to the 1,245-metre Cairn Gorm. Despite its relatively short distance it's a wild walk, perhaps the wildest in this book, and should not be underestimated. Good navigation and survival skills are needed up here, as well as top notch gear. It should be said that, albeit in November, it took this author two attempts to complete the walk due to the extreme wind speed – it later reached 81 miles an hour. In winter it's an even more serious proposition. Yet, on a good day, there is nothing like the Cairngorms for an amazing day Munro-bagging.

Back in the lively, outdoorsy town of Aviemore there are three fantastic pubs in which to toast your success.

Ski centre to Cairn Gorm

The ski centre called CairnGorm Mountain is a 20-minute drive or a 40-minute bus journey from the centre of Aviemore. As you snake up to the large car park there's a definite sense of mountain culture beginning – this could be an Alpine ski resort. Before you get this far be sure to check the Mountain Weather Information Service (mwis.org.uk) for the Cairngorms forecast. On the website you can also see observations from the weather station at the very summit of Cairn Gorm. In particular check the 'How windy?' section. Anything over 40mph and you should consider a pleasant afternoon in the Old Bridge Inn! Remember that once you are above Cairn Lochan it's likely to be very different from the car park. Also, fill out a route card at the Ranger Base … and be sure to let them know when you have returned.

So, from the car park you'll see the 'Winter of the Three' sculpture of 'chain people' skiing and snowboarding, walk past them and then along the clear path heading south-west. As you do the views to the north of Loch Morlich and the Queen's Forest really open out.

The route is largely cobbled for this part, with large boulders placed in the streams Allt Coire an t-Sneachda and later watercourses. The OS 1:25,000 Explorer map shows several paths carving off from the principal one we're on, but the 1:50,000 map simply displays the one we'll follow all the way up the ridge to just west of Cairn Lochan, as well as two earlier paths that go into Coire an t-Sneachda and into Coire an Lochain. If you do end up in Coire an Lochain then there is a path, albeit steep, up onto the ridge.

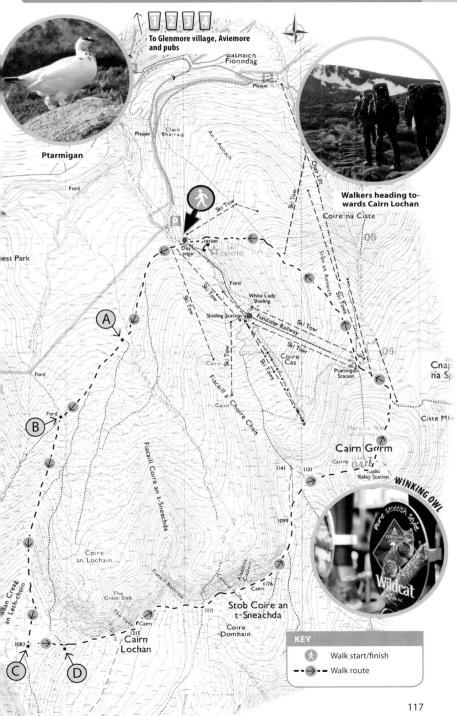

Ptarmigan

To Glenmore village, Aviemore
and pubs

Walkers heading towards Cairn Lochan

KEY

🚶 Walk start/finish

— ● → Walk route

At **A** 🕐 NH985051, just over Allt Coire an t-Sneachda, stay right as the path forks. Our destination is the ridge above Coire an Lochain. Cross over Allt Coire an Lochain at **B** 🕐 NH979044, and the path begins to gain the ridge.

Once on the ridge proper the path goes directly south. You should be on the highest part until it begins to flatten out, with a slight rise of land to your right. In clear weather the true scale and grandeur of the Cairngorms reveals itself. Around four kilometres ahead of you is Ben Macdui, the second highest mountain in Britain at 1,309 metres – before accurate maps, it was

Highland heather

thought that this could be the highest mountain (if it was, there'd be a lot more people there). It's also one of 18 Munros in the park. In October 1859, Queen Victoria climbed to the top of Ben Macdui, later writing: 'It had a sublime and solemn effect, so wild, so solitary – no one but ourselves and our little party there... I had a little whisky and water, as the people declared pure water would be too chilling.' We'll make no comment on the choice of drink (you did bring a hip-flask right?), but sublime, wild, and chilly are just as we'd recognise it now.

Almost more dramatic and one of Britain's most impressive mountain passes is the infamous Lairig Ghru. This vast, sweeping pass, carved out between Ben Macdui and Braeriach, Britain's third highest mountain, never fails to stop people in their tracks. Don't miss the opportunity to peer down into its depths and then up again at Braeriach to the south-west.

Slightly tricky navigation warning: once the path has flattened out you should be able to see the mountain rise sharply to the east up to Cairn Lochan. If you can see it, you'll also be able to see the small path that weaves up its slope and make a beeline towards it. If not, I suggest walking a little further along the path to **C** 🕐 NH976024 (as marked on the map) and walk directly east to pick up the path just at the point it rises up. It's a narrow path but discernible and you should hit it around **D** 🕐 NH979024. Follow it as it heads right and then directly up to the top of Cairn Lochan. As you rise up, it nears the cliff down into Coire an Lochain

CAIRNGORM FLORA AND FAUNA

The Cairngorm National Park has flora and fauna like no other place in Britain. Within its boundaries is a quarter of Scotland's native forest and one third of UK land above 600 metres. The plateau itself is Arctic-like and shares common characteristics with high-arctic Canada and northern Norway. This unique climate supports a huge variety of wildlife including red deer (impressive during the rut around October), pine marten, red squirrel, wild cat, otter and mountain hare. It also has a managed herd of reindeer – you'll pass the Reindeer Centre on the way to the start of this walk.

Birdlife that can be found high in the mountains includes the dotterel, snow bunting, snowy owl and the ptarmigan, a type of grouse that, like the mountain hare, turns white in winter. Raptors include osprey and golden eagle. The National Park also has important wetlands that support waders such as lapwings and red shank, as well as forests that are home to Scottish crossbill, crested tit and the capercaillie, the largest member of the grouse family.

– an impressive drop. There are two cairns at the top and the beginning of a gully between them. Be extremely careful in poor weather – there have been serious accidents here.

At the summit point of 1,215 metres, the path heads away from the cliff edge slightly and descends east to a narrow col between Cairn Lochan and Stob Coire an t-Sneachda. In poor weather be aware not to begin to walk down towards the north to the Fiacaill ridge.

Continuing east, you'll begin to rise up again towards Stob Coire an t-Sneachda and also come across the drop into Coire an t-Sneachda. It's common to see climbers poking out on the top here – there's great climbing, summer and winter.

A cairn, again close to the edge, marks the high point of 1,176 metres. The path is fairly clear here, and in good conditions you'll see the weather station at the top of Cairn Gorm ahead. Follow the path that hugs the top of the coire, then goes across a narrow col with Coire Raibeirt to your right. The path gradually curves north towards the top of the Fiacaill a Choire Chais, the ridge ahead of you (a path descends from here). By all means walk up to the 1,141-metre point, but a little earlier is a path that carves around to the east and directly across the rocky western flank towards Cairn Gorm's summit.

Climber on Stob Coire an t-Sneachda

Cairn Gorm to ski centre

Cairn Gorm, at 1,245 metres, is the sixth highest mountain in the UK and gives its name to the whole range. While the summit weather station and the ski runs below it diminish its wildness somewhat, there are still stunning views. It's one of the quickest Munros to bag too if you come up the route we're going

Snow and clouds on the Cairngorm plateau

Winking Owl

Old Bridge Inn

down. Nevertheless, this is also one of the windiest and most exposed places in the UK. On March 20, 1986, a British wind speed record of 173mph was reached. 100mph winds are common. As the development of the ski centre over the last 60 years attests, there's also a reasonably predictable amount of snowfall for the UK. The danger should not be underestimated – Britain's worst mountaineering disaster happened near here in November 1971 when five schoolchildren and an instructor died from exposure on the mountain after getting lost in white-out conditions.

From the summit of Cairn Gorm it's an easy walk back down to the ski centre – you can even take the funicular if you like. The route heads directly down to the Ptarmigan

station. While visitors to the station using the funicular railway can't leave the building to climb Cairn Gorm (when they could the summit became badly eroded), walkers can use it to descend. We're walking, of course. Either way, you need to head to the station. There's a cairned path that leads directly north towards it.

The route down is to the right of the building and is signposted as Windy Ridge Path. It descends Sròn an Aonaich down the north-west ridge to arrive at the ski centre car park. Sign off your route card at the Ranger Base.

The nearest place to get a good pint is at **1 Glenmore Lodge**, the National Outdoor Training Centre, a fabulous place where this author has done several courses. The Lochain Bar is a comfortable place to sit and relax surrounded by plenty of like-minded people. Behind the bar are some fine beers from the Cairngorm Brewery, based in Aviemore.

Back in Aviemore, there are three great pubs. Driving back into town, the **2 Old Bridge Inn** is the first you'll get to. This is a lovely pub with good food, great beers and a wide selection of whiskies. Not far away is the **3 Cairngorm Hotel**, and the **Cairn Bar**, a friendly local place with some good beers on tap.

Further along Grampian Road is the fantastic **4 Winking Owl**, popular with walkers and more of an Alpine-style lodge bar than a British pub. It's the de facto tap room for Cairngorm Brewery with a wide selection of its beers always available.

PUB INFORMATION

1 GLENMORE LODGE
Signposted from Glenmore Village, PH22 1QZ
01479 861256 • glenmorelodge.org.uk •
Opening hours: from 5pm daily

2 OLD BRIDGE INN
23 Dalfaber Road, Aviemore, PH22 1PU
01479 811137 • oldbridgeinn.co.uk •
Opening hours: 12-11 Mon-Thu; 12-1am Fri & Sat; 12-11 Sun

3 CAIRNGORM HOTEL
Grampian Road, Aviemore, PH22 1PE
01479 810233 • cairngorm.com •
Opening hours: 11-11 Mon-Sat; 12-10.30 Sun

4 WINKING OWL
123 Grampian Road, Aviemore, PH22 1RH
01479 812368 • thewinkingowl.co
Opening hours: 12-11 Mon-Thu; 11-1am Fri, Sat, 12.30-11 Sun

Lochnagar

It's not hard to understand why Queen Victoria and her beloved Albert bought Balmoral Castle on the eastern edge of the Cairngorms as a Highland retreat. Mountains rise dramatically all around and pockets of ancient woodland are dotted across the estate. It's been a favourite royal escape ever since. This walk is wholly within the well-managed Balmoral Estate near the pleasant town of Ballater and three great pubs. From the fascinating Balmoral Estate Visitor Centre, we climb up to one of Scotland's most spectacular Munros, Cac Càrn Beag on Lochnagar. As the vertiginous coire drops away to the north, this route heads back down, past huge waterfalls, to Loch Muick and Queen Victoria's hideaway house at Glas-allt-Shiel. Mountain hares, stags and ptarmigan crisscross this part of the Cairngorm Plateau, Britain's only Arctic landscape. Navigationally, it is fairly straightforward but up on the summit the weather can be wild; it's an Alpine Tundra Climate with an average high of just 9.4°C. Wrap up whatever the weather!

- ▶ **Start/finish:** Spittal of Glenmuick, Balmoral Estate Visitor Centre
- ▶ **Access:** Car from Ballater, buses in summer to Spittal of Glenmuick
- ▶ **Distance:** 11.5 miles (18.5km)
- ▶ **Ascent:** 3,097ft (944m)
- ▶ **Duration:** 5-8 hours
- ▶ **Fitness:**
- ▶ **Navigation:**
- ▶ **OS map:** Explorer OL53 *Lochnager, Glen Muick & Glen Clova*
- ▶ **Local attractions:** Balmoral Castle, Royal Lochnagar Distillery
- ▶ **THE PUBS:** Alexandra Hotel, Balmoral Bar, Glenaden Hotel all in Ballater
- ▶ **Timing tip:** If using the bus, be sure to check the times back from Spittal of Glenmuick.

Boat house by Loch Muick

Spittal of Glenmuick to Cac Càrn Beag

The start of this walk is a 20-minute drive out of Ballater at the Spittal of Glenmuick (Muick is pronounced 'mick'). Be wary of deer jumping out into the road. Parking is available beside the Balmoral Estate Visitor Centre (£4 cash only and all proceeds go to maintaining the footpaths and other work in the area). The visitor centre is managed by the Balmoral Ranger Service and is an excellent introduction to Lochnagar, its royal connections and especially the flora and fauna that inhabit the estate. Mountain hares are a fairly common sight (this author has seen several here at different times of year), and a couple of stuffed examples in the centre demonstrate the size of these handsome beasts. Otters, red squirrels, capercaillie and pine martens also make their home among these hills and woodland. In the winter keep an eye out for snow bunting, in spring dotterel can be seen while rare ring ouzels are found in summer. Many birds of prey can also be seen on the thermals around the estate including the Peregrine falcon, Golden eagle, buzzard and kestrel. Also be sure to check the advice about deer stalking, but you should be fine on the paths.

The visitor centre at the Spittal of Glenmuick is the site of an old farmstead and inn dating back to the 15th century. The inn or hospice was run by monks who provided food and shelter for travellers, and the remains of a farming community here can be seen on a small walk. It's an unforgiving land to farm, and today it is grouse shooting and deer stalking that provide much of the income for the estate.

So, let's begin the walk. From the visitor centre, walk past one set of farm buildings and take the first right. A sign marks the Lochnagar Path that we're following (we return along the Loch Muick Path). In the distance you'll see a couple of cottages at Allt-na-giubhsaich (where Queen Victoria

River Muick

Woodland by Allt-na-giubhsaich

Crossing Allt-na-giubhsaich

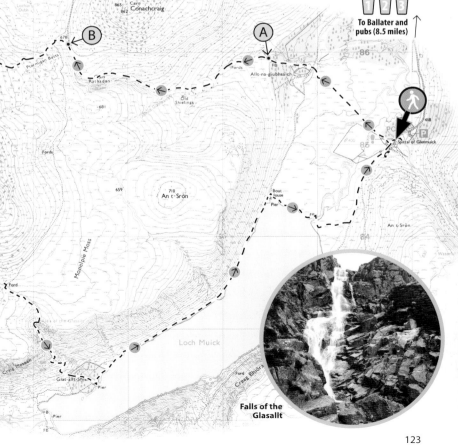

To Ballater and pubs (8.5 miles)

Falls of the Glasallt

123

Summit indicator on Lochnagar

path west until you emerge onto the moorland at **A** 🧭 NO294859. A wide, clear path then rises fairly gently west and then north around Conachcraig. Before long there is a burn to ford. It's usually okay to step across some stones at the point where the path meets the burn, otherwise, you may need to head upstream a little. Always take care crossing water, no matter how benign it seems.

As the path arches around Conachcraig, the moorland opens up, and on a clear day you should be able to see Lochnagar rising steeply ahead. As the track curves north, at the col between Conachcraig and Meikle Pap, take the path that forks off to the left at **B** 🧭 NO273860. It dips down and then rises increasingly steeply towards Lochnagar. On the right, you'll clearly see the subsidiary Munro of Meikle Pap – worth bagging if you're up this way. Before you get to the col between Meikle Pap and Lochnagar, there's a small memorial just off the path dedicated

and Albert stayed) and that's our first destination. Walk along the wide track and across the footbridge near the beginning of the River Muick that feeds into the Dee at Ballater. Ahead is the 850-metre Conachcraig. To the left is a larger house and almost straight ahead is a smaller cottage. The Lochnagar Path passes just to the left of this smaller building and into woodland. It is signposted.

This lovely stretch of woodland has a bouncy undergrowth – follow the rough

**Lochnagar's summit
trig point**

Woodland around Loch Muick

to Bill Stuart, a climber who died on a Lochnagar buttress in 1953. From the col, at **C** 🔍 NO259858, you'll clearly see the body of water known as Lochnagar that gives this area its name. Above it are the foreboding buttresses rising up to Cac Càrn Mòr and the Munro of Cac Càrn Beag.

The first ascent of Lochnagar was a winter climb up the left-hand branch of the Black Spout by William Douglas and John Henry Gibson in 1893. The nearby Douglas-Gibson Gully bears their names after a thwarted attempt. In fact, it wasn't successfully climbed until 1950. Today, this is one of the most popular spots for winter climbing in the Cairngorms as it holds the snow and ice very well.

Back to our slightly easier walk, from the col a clear path runs up above Lochnagar. It is steep but fairly easy to follow with only a small section where the path is hard to discern as you clamber over rocks. This is really a walk for the summer, but if you are attempting this in the snow, be aware that Lochnagar holds notorious cornices.

Once the path levels out, it follows the

Chaffinch

top of the corrie edge all the way around to Cac Càrn Mòr. Our path follows the route that drops slightly down from the edge as it's easier to navigate, especially in bad weather, but the destination is the same. It's a very steep drop into the corrie and several climbers have died here. Following our route is straightforward even in poor conditions as the path is clear and there are some cairns marking the route. But up here my advice is to always take a compass bearing, especially in the cloud. Another advantage of ascending this way is that you'll see the junction for the return route at **D** 🔍 NO248852. Take note of this, but turn right towards Cac Càrn Mòr. There's a short few steps up and then you head along a wide path across a broad plateau. You'll see the large cairn on top of a tor, turn right toward this at **E** 🔍 NO244856. There are two tors up here, similar to those you'd find on Dartmoor – one before you on Cac Càrn Mòr and a much bigger one on the summit of Cac Càrn Beag. These stacks of granite are the result of weathering between 65 and 2.4 million years ago according to information at the visitor centre. The Cairngorms is one of the world's oldest mountain ranges and is the product of a vast collision between continents that melted rock, which then bubbled up and hardened some 415 million years ago.

Mind duly blown, time for the final assault to Cac Càrn Beag. From the cairn, follow the wide, clear footpath down and then up again to the tor and summit trig point. There's also an indicator here, constructed in 1924 by the Cairngorm Club, showing the hills around. Count yourself lucky if you can see any!

Cac Càrn Beag to Spittal of Glenmuick

From the summit, retrace your steps back to the cairn at Cac Càrn Mòr. Care is needed here as it's easy to become disorientated in bad weather. From the cairn, descend along the path, turning almost immediately left. Don't go down the path that continues

straight down past another large cairn, we're heading south-east, to the junction at **D** NO248852 and down alongside the Glas Allt stream that empties into Loch Muick. This is a spectacular path that descends down a steeply sided mountain, with views straight down to Loch Muick, but the best part of the path is at the end. It's perhaps the noise you'll hear before you see the view, but the Falls of the Glasallt are a wonderful sight. The path is exciting too. On windy days it can seem as though the falls are flowing up the valley, and you'll get some of the spray as you clamber down. It's a steep zigzag by the side of the falls, but there are plenty of points for you to stop and admire this feature. The route then follows on slightly above Glas Allt, before weaving down to a stone wall. You'll see it has been knocked down here but this is the route. Hop over the stones and onto a path. There's a wooden bridge on the left, but before you cross it follow a small track

Bridge over Glas Allt

Bothy at Glas-allt-Shiel

that leads down to Glas-allt-Shiel, an old Victorian house that you will now be able to see. And by 'Victorian' I actually mean ordered by the Queen herself.

There is something a little spooky about this boarded up hunting lodge Glas-allt-Shiel. It was built in 1868 after the death of Prince Albert and consequently became known as the 'Widow's House'. It was used by the Queen when she was on her walks out of Balmoral, for royal hunters and for a spectacular picnic setting. It was one of a number of hideaways the Queen had. It is still used occasionally by Prince Charles, who has been known to invite climbers into the bothy for a 'wee dram'.

ROYAL RETREAT

All of the land covered in this walk is within the Balmoral Estate that is privately owned by the royal family, and not the property of the Crown. Balmoral Castle was bought by Prince Albert in 1852 and it became one of Victoria and Albert's favourite places. It has been equally favoured by more recent monarchs, including the current royal family who regularly visits the castle, especially during the summer. Queen Victoria, in her diary, wrote of Balmoral: 'All seemed to breathe freedom and peace, and to make one forget the world and its sad turmoils'. It is said the surrounding landscape reminded Prince Albert of his woodland home in Germany and it was a place for rest and relaxation away from the pressures of London life. The Balmoral Estate has subsequently grown to more than 50,000 acres, much of it a working landscape, with grouse shooting and farming the main activities. Prince Charles is a regular visitor here and generally stays at Birkhall, one of the buildings on the estate. He even set his children's book, *The Old Man of Lochnagar*, here. The story is based on one Prince Charles used to tell to his younger brothers. In the story, the old man lives in a cave under Lochnagar.

Glas-Allt-Shiel, the 'Widow's House'

Alexandra Hotel

Barrel Lounge at the Glenaden Hotel

It looks boarded up, but you can actually stay here, well, in one of the outbuildings. This is probably the most remarkable bothy in Scotland. Bothies are shelters, often in disused shepherd's huts, that can be used by hillwalkers and climbers for a night. This one is around the back of the main building. It's little more than a room on the ground floor with a fire and then a mezzanine area for sleeping. The Dundee University Rucksack Club maintains it. There's a clear 'bothy code' for staying, for example leaving the place clean and tidy, and ensuring there's always some dry kindling for the next visitor. The Mountain Bothies Association, although not responsible for this particular bothy, provides an excellent online resource about bothies at mountainbothies.org.uk.

From the Widow's House, it's a very straightforward walk back to the visitor centre at the Spittal of Glenmuick. A wide track leads around the northern side of the loch (although if you want to extend the walk even further, there is a path around the other side, however, both avalanches and rock slides have been known here). At the end of the Loch are a boathouse and small pier. Bear right here along the clear path beside the end of the loch. Continue along this path, crossing a footbridge and rising gently to meet another path. Turn left here and straight back to the visitor centre.

Back in Ballater, there are three excellent pubs, all with quite different atmospheres. The **1** **Alexandra Hotel** is a popular spot for lunch and dinner with a beer, but there is a small bar to sit at as well. It's a *Good Beer Guide* regular and there were two great beers from the Cairngorm Brewery on when I visited. The **2** **Balmoral Bar** is a popular pub with a pool room, darts and a couple of large TVs. On the bar there's always one handpumped beer, plus on my visit a couple of interesting kegged craft beers were on offer too. Across the town square, behind the church, is another *Good Beer Guide* regular, the **3** **Glenaden Hotel** and the bar called the Barrel Lounge. It's a friendly place, with three changing beers and always a dark beer.

PUB INFORMATION

1 Alexandra Hotel
12 Bridge Square, Ballater, AB35 5QJ
01339 755376 • alexandrahotelballater.co.uk •
Opening hours: 11-2.30, 5-midnight; 11-midnight Fri & Sat

2 Balmoral Bar
1 Netherley Place, Ballater, AB35 5QE
01339 755462
Opening hours: 11-midnight (1am Thu-Sat); 12.30-midnight Sun

3 Glenaden Hotel
6 Church Square, Ballater, AB35 5NE
01339 755488 •
Opening hours: 11-1 (midnight Mon-Wed)

Innerleithen to Peebles

This walk has it all: huge rolling hills, historical interest, fantastic pubs and even a brewery to look around. Scotland's border country is often overlooked by hillwalkers, but unfairly, as this is some of Scotland's most beautiful countryside, offering deep valleys, ancient forests and lofty hills, often scattered with the remnants of ancient settlements. This is something walkers along the 212-mile Southern Upland Way know well of course, and our route follows a brief part of that. It also follows a few miles of the Cross Borders Drove Road. We start out in the village of Innerleithen and soon stop at Traquair House, the oldest continually inhabited house in Scotland and home to a brewery. The route then climbs onto the ancient drove road, before the long ridgeline descent into the bustling town of Peebles, home to several great pubs.

▶ **Start/finish:** Innerleithen/ Peebles

▶ **Access:** Regular buses between Innerleithen, Peebles and Edinburgh

▶ **Distance:** 10.5 miles (17km)

▶ **Ascent:** 1,650ft (503m)

▶ **Duration:** 4-6 hours

▶ **Fitness:** 👢👢

▶ **Navigation:** 🧭🧭

▶ **OS map:** Explorer 337 *Peebles & Innerleithen*

▶ **Local attractions:** Traquair House, Glentress Forest mountain biking

▶ **THE PUBS:** Traquair Arms Hotel, Innerleithen; Bridge Inn (Trust), Cross Keys, Crown Hotel, Peebles

▶ **Timing tip:** If Traquair House is open, then be sure to leave time to look around.

The Tweed Bridge at Peebles

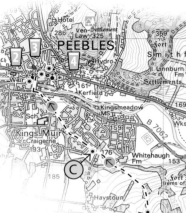

Cardrona Forest

Innerleithen to Kirkhope Law

The 🚶 **Traquair Arms Hotel** is as good as anywhere to start in Innerleithen, especially if you're staying here or you need to return on the short hop back along the road from Peebles. It's a good pub, notable for the fact it always has flavoursome brews from the Traquair House Brewery. Innerleithen itself is worth a short wander round. According to Sir Walter Scott, in his novel *St Ronan's Well*, there's been a town here since AD737 and it was founded by St Ronan who arrived at the confluence of rivers in a coracle. Whether it's true or not, the village would have certainly been on important routes for pilgrims, monks and drovers travelling on the River Tweed or by it. Innerleithen is also close to Traquair, long an important country house with a remarkable history.

Quair Water

From the pub, walk south along Traquair Road out of the village and over the bridge crossing the River Tweed. This 197-mile river that flows across Scotland's border regions and into northern England is well known for its salmon fishing. In a roundabout way, it also gives its name to the tweed material; tweel was the original name, but the story goes that there was a misunderstanding over a letter from a Hawick firm (not too far from Innerleithen) in which 'tweel' was misread as 'tweed' after the river. From then on the name stuck. And if there's anywhere you're likely to see some tweed it's on the huge aristocratic estates of the Scottish Borders.

There is some road walking at the beginning of this route, so care is needed, although we've avoided any busy roads. Over the bridge, follow the road around to the right, signposted to Traquair House, rising gently. If Traquair House is open, don't miss the chance to see it (see box page 132).

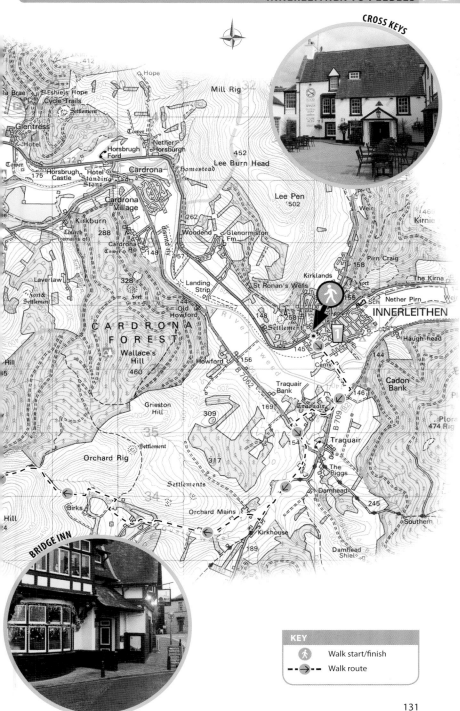

CROSS KEYS

Hope

Mill Rig

la Brae
PC
Eshiels Hope
Cycle Trails
Settlement

Glentress

Hotel

Tower

Nether
Horsburgh

Horsburgh
Ford

452

Lee Burn Head

Tower

175

Horsburgh
Castle

Hotel
Standing
Stone

Cardrona

Homestead

Lee Pen
502

Weir

Kirnie

Cardrona
Village

262

Kirkburn

Church
(remains of)

288

Woodend

Glenormiston
Fm

Pirn Craig

158

The Kirna

Cardrona
Tower Ho

148

157

Kirklands

Sch

Nether Pirn

Weir

Laverlaw

328

Fort

St Ronan's Wells

Fort

155

INNERLEITHEN

Fort &
Settlement

Hill

144

Old
Howford

148

258

Settlement

145

Haugh-head

Hill

**C A R D R O N A
F O R E S T**

Wallace's
Hill

460

Howford

156

Camp

144

Cadon
Bank

Traquair
Bank

Grieston
Hill

309

169

Traquair

146

Plora
474 Rig

Orchard Rig

Settlement

317

154

Traquair

Settlements

The
Riggs

Hill

Birks

34

Orchard Mains

Kirkhouse

Damhead

245

Southern

189

Damhead
Shiel

BRIDGE INN

At the gatehouse, marked as 'Lodge' on the OS map, turn right into the estate. Follow the road around to the left and across a bridge over Quair Water. The splendour of this 15th-century house is said to have influenced the Scottish Baronial style. Brewery tours and tastings are available if arranged in advance. There's also a restaurant and shop if you want to buy some beer, or some Traquair Ale shampoo.

You won't miss it, but opposite the house is the main drive. Walk up here, past the shop and the 1745 Cottage Restaurant to the road

Along the old drove road

TRAQUAIR HOUSE

Traquair House is Scotland's oldest inhabited house. It was built as a royal hunting lodge and has been lived in for more than 900 years. In 1491, the Earl of Buchan gave the estate to his son James Stewart who became the 1st Laird of Traquair. The house you see today dates back to between the 1500s and 1600s. During this period the family became part of the political elite and Mary Queen of Scots visited in 1566. By the mid 1600s, the family had returned to their Catholic roots and supported the Jacobite cause. The Bear Gates, which our walk goes past, were built in 1739. They were closed for good in 1745 after a visit from Bonnie Prince Charlie. The 5th Earl promised they would never be opened again until the Stuarts returned to the throne and so the gates remain closed. Today, the 21st Lady of Traquair, Catherine Maxwell Stuart, occupies the house.

The house is largely open to the public who can explore its rooms and the artwork on its walls. Equally interesting are the gardens, including a large, hedged maze and sculptures in the 'Old Walled Garden'. Also on site are a restaurant, chapel, shops, craft workshops and, of course, the brewery.

Traquair House Brewery dates back to the 1700s and made beer for the household. By the early 1800s, beer was no longer being made, but the brewery was never taken apart. In the 1960s, Peter Maxwell Stuart, Catherine's father, began brewing again.

Brewery tours take place throughout the year and include tastings in the 18th-century dining room. The wonderful ales are available to buy in the brewery shop.

at the top. Turn right briefly to have a look at the Bear Gates. These were closed in 1745 following the visit of Bonnie Prince Charlie. The 5th Earl then promised that they would never be opened again until the Stuarts returned to the throne. They're still closed.

Turn back along the lane heading south-east, and just over the bridge turn right along a small lane to an old mill. Continue south-west to Kirkhouse – it's along the road, but this is also part of the Southern Upland Way. Take a right signposted to 'Glen House' and trot down to Orchard Mains farm. Follow the lane around to the left and continue for 1.5 miles until you see a fork in the road and a gatehouse. Follow the principal lane on the right fork until you reach a junction and a three-way fingerpost. We're taking a right turn and taking the Cross Borders Drove Road to Peebles. At the end of the track, another small post has the Cross Borders Drove Road badge on it. Follow that left and down to a gate. Turn left through the gate and start the long climb up and around Birks Hill cutting across open moorland. The path touches the corner of a plantation, before a lovely stretch across open fields. At **A** 🕒 NT276340, you'll come across another corner of the plantation. Follow this around to a gate. Then take the path along the wall north-east to the high

Statue at Traquair House

point of the day, Kirkhope Law at 1,761ft (537m).

The Cross Borders Drove Road is a 51-mile long-distance trail and part of 'Scotland's Great Trails'. It starts at the town of Hawick, a place well known for knitwear, and goes towards Edinburgh ending at the Pentland Hills (see Walk 17). For more than two centuries, cattle and sheep were driven across this landscape between markets known as 'trysts'. The practice fizzled out during the middle of the 19th century, but the pathways, like all across Britain, remain.

Kirkhope Law to Peebles

From Kirkhope Law it's an easy descent into Peebles, and the town itself should soon come into view. The path undulates along a wide ridge over Kailzie Hill and high above Glensax Burn down to your left. It really is a

Looking back towards Hundleshope Heights from the old drove road

Bridge Inn

Cross Keys

beautiful stretch of pathway. By the time you round Craig Head, Peebles should be clear. At **B** 🕙 NT268381, take a look on the right for the remains of an ancient hillfort. Iron Age pottery has been found in this area. The drove road falls now towards Haystoun Burn, which it crosses in a woodland area. At **C** 🕙 NT259392 you'll come out onto Glen Road, which you can follow into the town. It turns into Springhill Road, before crossing the Tweed. On the left hand side just on the other side of the river is the **2** **Bridge Inn**.

What's not to like about the Bridge Inn? This is a fantastic pub, so much so, it's hard to move on anywhere else. The friendly

staff are not only entertaining, they're knowledgeable about the beers too. There's a log-burning stove to dry your boots by while you admire the beers on tap (which included the marvellous Jarl from Fyne Ales on my last visit). There's also a book made by the staff showing the highlights of Peebles and the area around (as well as a fair amount of whim).

The pub was first opened in 1896, but many in the town know it as the Trust. As the local council widened the bridge over the Tweed, the Tweedside Inn, as it was then known, was rented to the East of Scotland Public House Trust, hence the Trust name.

If you can drag yourself away, there are two other pubs often listed in the *Good Beer Guide*. The **3** **Crown Hotel** has a long, narrow bar that is very popular and often busy. There's one changing beer that is usually a local one. Also recommended is the large **4** **Cross Keys**, an old coaching inn that is now a Wetherspoon's pub.

PUB INFORMATION

1 **TRAQUAIR ARMS HOTEL**
Traquair Rd, Innerleithen EH44 6PD
01896 830229 • traquairarmshotel.co.uk • 🛏
Opening hours: 11-11 (midnight Fri & Sat);
12-11.30 Sun

2 **BRIDGE INN (TRUST)**
Portbrae, Peebles, EH45 8AW
01721 720589
Opening hours: 11-midnight (1am Thu-Sat);
12-midnight Sun

3 **CROWN HOTEL**
High Street, Peebles, EH45 8SW
01721 720239 • crownhotelpeebles.co.uk • 🛏
Opening hours: 11-midnight (1am Thu-Sat)

4 **CROSS KEYS**
Northgate, Peebles, EH45 8RS
01721 723467 • 🛏
Opening hours: 7am-midnight (1am Fri & Sat)

Cross Keys

Pentland Hills circular

WALK 17

It's easy to underestimate the Pentland Hills, a range of gently arching hills south-west of Edinburgh, both in terms of the challenge they provide and also the beauty they offer. Be under no illusion though, this is a real mountain day out, reaching a height of 1,880ft (573m) with some steep climbing. The walker will be rewarded with endless views over the city of Edinburgh, across the Scottish Borders and north into Midlothian. The area is a playground for nearby residents enjoying the scenery from two wheels or two feet. This route leaves from the town of Balerno, where there's a pub well regarded by the local CAMRA branch with more options nearby. Its proximity and easy access to Edinburgh means that a wealth of some of Scotland's best pubs is never more than half an hour away.

▶ **Start/finish:** Harlaw House Visitor Centre

▶ **Access:** Bus numbers 44 and 44a from Edinburgh stop in Balerno

▶ **Distance:** 9.5 miles (15.5km)

▶ **Ascent:** 2,316ft (706m)

▶ **Duration:** 4-6 hours

▶ **Fitness:** 👟👟

▶ **Navigation:** 🧭🧭

▶ **OS maps:** Explorer 344 *Pentland Hills*

▶ **Local attractions:** Edinburgh city centre sights

▶ **THE PUBS:** Grey Horse, Balerno; Juniper Green Inn, Juniper Green

▶ **Timing tip:** If you're heading back to Edinburgh by bus, check the times carefully.

Looking over Black Springs

Harlaw House Visitor Centre

Harlaw House Visitor Centre to Carnethy Hill

The Pentland Hills Regional Park is popular among outdoor enthusiasts escaping the city and understandably so. Although only around 20 miles in length, there are 60 miles of trails with routes varying from those high up in the hills to ambles around the reservoirs.

We start our trail at Harlaw House Visitor Centre (open 11-3.30 Mon-Fri; 11.30-3 Sat-Sun) where there is a large car park. If you are arriving by bus from Edinburgh city centre, walk out of Balerno along the Harlaw Road until you reach a sharp left turn. From here you'll see a little wooded track that is signposted, and this will lead you to the visitor centre.

Farmland by Harlaw Reservoir

From the visitor centre, start walking along the wide path around the eastern side of Harlaw Reservoir following the little blue sign with a squirrel. This is one of 13 reservoirs in the Pentland Hills Regional Park and was built to power the mills that were mostly dedicated to paper, but also produced grain and snuff. Malleny Mills, on Harlaw Road between Balerno and the visitor centre, was a flax and grain mill.

The path arrives at a stone stile where there's a fingerpost marked 'Black Springs', our first destination of the day. Cross the stile and head right and then immediately left. Go through the metal gate that doesn't have a signpost and walk along the path down

KEY

👤 Walk start/finish

- - → - - Walk route

The path around
Black Hill

towards Black Springs. You'll come out at
part of the Threipmuir Reservoir that supplies
Edinburgh with water, just below a couple
of springs that feed it. Turn right along
the frequently boggy track to a causeway
across the reservoir and then walk towards
a small stone hut on the other side at **A** 👤
NT187640. Head up a sharp, rocky path to
the right of the hut and south-west, along
the side of the great mass of Black Hill.

The Pentland Hills were born out of violent
volcanic activity millions of years ago. The
rounded look of the hills suggests their age
and the fact that glaciers and huge ice flows
sheared off any jagged aspect. As you traverse
Black Hill, below you to the west you may be
able to make out Bavelaw Castle, a historic
house built in the 16th century. Mary, Queen
of Scots and James VI both stayed there.

As you round the south-west end of Black
Hill, the muddy path narrows and the hill
drops dramatically down to your right. Care
is needed here. Keep going however, slowly
downhill to Logan Burn at the bottom.

Hut and stile below Black Hill

Here, the true drama and intricacy of the hills can be seen. Since ancient times, they have protected their inhabitants. Celtic tribes settled in the hills and they would have witnessed the arrival of the Romans with whom, according to the Pentland Hills website, they co-existed as the Roman army built their base at Cramond, directly north of where we stand. From the 12th century, stag-hunting parties were common in the hills, led on some occasions by Robert the Bruce.

At the bottom of the descent, continue east over and along the burn until you see a cottage known as the Howe at **B** NT190620 and the head of Loganlee Reservoir that connects to the larger Glencorse Reservoir.

We're heading up, however, to Carnethy Hill. There are a couple of ways to get up this 1,880ft (573m) hill, both steep. Perhaps the least difficult route is up to the col between Carnethy Hill and Scald Law, the highest hill in the park at 1,900ft (579m). From the Howe, follow the fingerpost marked Penicuik to start the biggest climb of the day. It's a short, but steep walk up to the col at **C** NT195615. If you're feeling particularly energetic then you can also knock off Scald Law, a steep half a kilometre from the cross roads. If not, then turn left and head generally east along a clear path up to Carnethy Hill. It's a beautiful spot, but why let me describe it when we can turn to Sir Walter Scott who wrote:

BATTLE OF RULLION GREEN

It was the defining moment of the Pentland Rising. It was the first time the Covenanters, a Scottish Presbyterian movement that sought to make their doctrine the sole religion in Scotland, had armed themselves to fight for their movement. After the restoration of Charles II to Scotland in 1660, episcopacy was restored dashing the hopes of the Covenant-ers. However, rebel ministers continued to preach at secret locations in the countryside, including in the Pentland Hills. These meet-ings were banned and preachers punished as a capital offence. It was too much for the Covenanters who, for the first time, and with little planning, took up arms and marched

towards Edinburgh across the Pentland Hills. The poorly armed Covenanters were met by a much larger Royalist force led by Sir Thomas Dalziel. A headstone by the battlefield, erected in 1738, reveals the outcome: 'Here and near to this place lyes the Reverend Mr John Crookshank and Mr Andrew M'cormick ministers of the Gospel and About fifty other true covenanted Presbyterians who were killed in this place in their own Inocent self de-fence and defence of the covenanted work of Reformation By Thomas Dalzeel of Bins upon the 28 of november 1666 Rev 12. 11 Erected September 28, 1738.' *(Transcription provided by www.thereformation.info)*

*'I think I never saw anything
more beautiful than
the ridge of Carnethy against
a clear frosty sky,
with its peaks and varied slopes.
The hills glowed like purple amethyst;
the sky glowed topaz and
vermillion colours.
I never saw a finer screen than Pentland,
considering that it is neither rocky
or elevated.'*

Actually, as you rise up towards the summit, Carnethy Hill does turn somewhat rocky, or perhaps stony would be more accurate. The summit cairn can be seen, alongside a range of stone shelters. It is thought that parts of these cairns are ancient, and certainly, other archaeological remains have been found on the hills. Down below to the left, you'll see clearly how Loganlee Reservoir turns again into a burn and then towards Glencorse Reservoir.

Carnethy Hill to Harlaw House Visitor Centre

From the summit, trot down north-east to the col and the fence. Go through the gate and then up to Turnhouse Hill at 1,660ft

The Howe

(506m). There's a cairn at **D** ⊗ NT212626 on the wide summit.

From here, if you look down to your right, below you is a battlefield, marked on the OS map. It is the site of the Battle of Rullion Green where more than 50 Covenanters were killed by troops under General Tam Dalziel in 1666 (see box opposite). From the summit cairn, continue along the ridge to the secondary top at **E** ⊗ NT214630 before following the clear path directly east and down. It's a pleasant jaunt down to the plantations at the bottom beside the Glencorse Burn that leads out of Glencorse Reservoir. The path undulates slowly down, and as you reach a gate at the bottom, turn right towards the road. You'll see a car park and a visitor centre a little further east along the road. We're turning left onto the road to rise back up towards Glencorse Reservoir. It's a paved track to allow access to large

**Looking back towards Carnethy
Hill from Turnhouse Hill**

Grey Horse (above and right)

vehicles relating to the reservoir, but not open to the public and therefore usually quiet. As the road rises north-west, there are great views of the mountains you've just descended from.

The road rises up to Glen Cottage right by the dam, and then alongside the reservoir itself, a popular destination for boat fly fishing. Glencorse Reservoir was built between 1820 and 1824 and submerged St Catherine's Chapel.

Just over the Kirk Bridge, go through a large metal gate on the right at **F** NT215640 and onto a wide path that leads all the way back to the Harlaw House Visitor Centre. The path rises up through Maiden's Cleugh to the pass and a gate at **G** NT203649. Over the brow, you'll see the path winding down just over a mile to the car park a little north of the Harlaw House Visitor Centre. It's a very straightforward walk to the car park. Once there, turn left at the wall in front of the car park and head along the wide track to the visitor centre. At the

end, you'll see the signpost that leads back through the wooded track to Harlaw Road and then onto Balerno.

Time for a pint then? Fortunately, there's a great option in Balerno, the **1 Grey Horse**. This is a traditional village pub that dates back to the 18th century. It is a pub of two halves, with a newly refurbished dining section plus a down-to-earth bar with a fire and original wood panelling. Above the fireplace is a copy of the minutes from the first meeting of the Balerno Burns Club, known as 'Let it Blaw', held here in 1881 (when the pub was called Henderson's Inn). The club, which is still going, is dedicated to celebrating the life and works of Scotland's national bard, Robert Burns. The annual January supper includes toasts, songs and recitations, as well as the 'hilarity and harmony' recorded in the report of their first gathering back in 1881.

There's certainly plenty of beer on offer to celebrate with. On my visit beers included those from Harviestoun and the new Cross Borders Brewery based in nearby Dalkeith (established in June 2016). In the dining area there's an excellent menu focussing on local ingredients.

Before heading all the way back into Edinburgh, it's worth stopping at the **2 Juniper Green Inn** in Juniper Green. This is a cosy little pub in a building dating back to the late 1800s. It's a proper community pub and has a good selection of beers from around Britain.

PUB INFORMATION

1 GREY HORSE
20 Main Street, Balerno, EH14 7EH
0131 449 2888 • greyhorsebalerno.com
Opening hours: 11-11 (midnight Fri, Sat)

2 JUNIPER GREEN INN
542 Lanark Road, Juniper Green, EH14 5EL
0131 458 5395
Opening hours: 11-midnight (11 Mon & Tue); 12.30-11 Sun

Wales

Snowdon via Y Lliwedd

Snowdon: The king of mountains in England and Wales. It is a fantastically complex jumble of Alpine-like arêtes, spurs and cwms (cirques, or scooped valleys) all leading to the pyramidal peak of Snowdon or Yr Wyddfa. This North Wales mountain is en-shrouded in folklore, in natural history and in tales of human perseverance, with its cliff edges, remote tarns and ancient pathways echoing stories of bravery and tragedy. There is no other mountain in the British Isles that holds so much interest. Far from being a straight-up straight-down mountain, there are numerous ways to reach the summit from almost every angle and for most abilities, from the relatively straight-forward Llanberis Path to the knife-edge ridge of Crib Goch (and even by train!).

WALK 18

▸ **Start/finish:** Pen-y-Pass car park

▸ **Access:** Hourly Snowdon Sherpa buses between Llanberis and Betws-y-Coed in summer, every two hours in winter

▸ **Duration:** 4–6hrs

▸ **Distance:** 7 miles (11.5km)

▸ **Ascent:** 3,251ft (991m)

▸ **Fitness:**

▸ **Navigation:**

▸ **OS map:** Explorer OL17 Snowdon/Yr Wyddfa

▸ **Key attractions:** Zipworld, Bounce Below, Snowdon Mountain Railway

▸ **THE PUBS:** Pen-y-Gwryd Hotel, Nant Gwynant; Plas-y-Brenin, Tyn-y-Coed Inn, both Capel Curig

▸ **Timing tip:** Be sure to check the last bus times from Pen-y-Pass

The mighty Y Lliwedd was used for Everest training

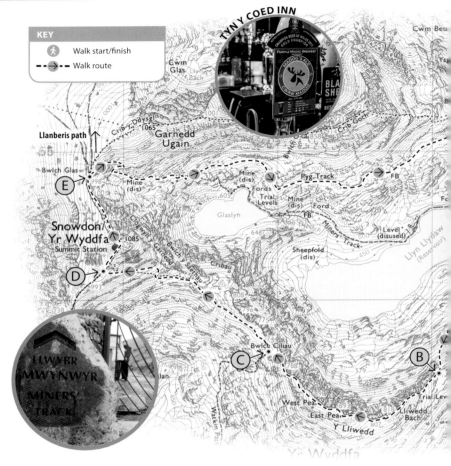

KEY

🚶 Walk start/finish

--→-- Walk route

The route described here adds extra spice by climbing up to the sharp peak of Y Lliwedd, remarkably quiet even on a nice Sunday in summer, before the final pull up to Snowdon's summit. It's a mildly technical route with a little bit of scrambling and best for experienced hillwalkers. We then return to Pen-y-Pass car park via the Pyg Track. But beware of Snowdon: this is a huge mountain and the weather can be very different on the top than in the valleys. Always check the warden's report – particularly important if it is cold. Both the top of the Pyg Track and the top of the Watkin Path can be treacherous in ice and snow. Always have a backup plan. Again, this walk is described for summer conditions.

Back down from the mountain there are a number of interesting options for a beer, including the base for many of the early Everest training expeditions, the Pen-y-Gwryd Hotel.

Pen-y-Pass car park to Y Lliwedd

🚶 It's always best to get an early start in the mountains, and this is especially true on Snowdon. Not only can you be in the pub earlier, but there's more chance of you being able to park at Pen-y-Pass car park. It gets full early on weekends. The price is £10

Snowdon above Llyn Llydaw

for all-day parking. There's a small visitor centre, cafe and toilets. Across the road is YHA Snowdon Pen-y-Pass, a good place for a coffee. Pen-y-Pass car park is at 350 metres and we're heading up to the Snowdon summit at 1,085 metres, the joint third highest summit in the British Isles. It's a long, amazing day ahead.

Our route starts along the Miners' Track, one of the more popular routes to the summit. There are two exits out of the car park and the Miners' Track is out of the south side of the lower car park. A large stone next to the wall marks the start:

'Llwybr y Mwynwyr, Miners' Track'. Go through the lovely iron gates and onto the wide path. We're taking this bridleway to Llyn Llydaw, before breaking off to Y Lliwedd.

The path rises above Llyn Teyrn to the left and beyond that to a prominent pipeline that directs water from Llyn Llydaw to the Cwm Dyli, the world's oldest hydro-electric power station that feeds into a national grid. It was commissioned in 1906 and is still going today. James Bond fans will recognise it from *The World is Not Enough*. Here you'll also notice some of the left-over mining infrastructure that gives this path its name.

As you see Llyn Llydaw, thought to be one of the coldest lakes in the country, keep an eye out for a little green hut and a path leading off to it at **A**  **SH634545**. Turn left onto this path and follow it around the southern edge of Llyn Llydaw. (The causeway was built in 1853 for a copper mine. When the level of the lake was lowered they found a prehistoric dug-out canoe.) You'll cross a footbridge as the path begins to climb in earnest and away from the lake. The pull up to Y Lliwedd has started. The path here is a good one and fairly easy to follow at first.

The steep eastern flanks of Y Lliwedd, almost always looking forebodingly dark, were used by George Mallory in training for his ill-fated Everest attempt in 1924. Exercises also took place here for the successful 1953 British Mount Everest Expedition (see box).

The Snowdon massif taken from near Plas y Brenin

It's another never-ending staircase up to the eastern flank of Y Lliwedd that gets steeper and steeper. Although not a scramble, there are some places you'll need to put down a steadying hand. There is a fairly steep drop at some points. You'll also need to be very aware of the path, especially as you hit some bedrock and the path momentarily disappears. Usually taking the easiest looking route puts you back on the path in no time. Note that in some cases the path zig zags up and behind you briefly. At **B** **SH630535**, the ground levels out and there's a very large cairn.

From here, a fairly clear path then leads over the summit ridge of Y Lliwedd. Again, it is steep in places, and you'll no doubt have noticed an extremely long drop down to your right. At some points, the path gets very close to the edge. There's usually a place to go not so close, but a trip isn't an option. Some prefer to scramble over the very top of the ridge, but there is a loose path just to the left. It's also worth keeping an eye on your compass – it's generally north-west once you've reached the East Peak of Y Lliwedd. The path undulates all around the ridge with the high point being at 898 metres at the West Peak.

THE EVEREST OF WALES

The history of early British expeditions to climb Everest is indelibly linked to Snowdon. It is on the dark, vertiginous cliffs of Y Lliwedd and Clogwyn Du'r Arddu where Edmund Hillary and, before him, George Mallory and his climbing partner Andrew Irvine trained. YHA Snowdon Pen-y-Pass was once the Gorphwysfa Hotel, an infamous haunt of climbing legends who often interspersed their climbing with riotous evenings in the hotel. Along with George Mallory, the guestbook includes names of climbing legends such as the Abraham Brothers and Geoffrey Winthrop Young who, along with his climbing cohorts, would arrive from Cambridge on annual Easter gatherings from 1903 until the 1930s. There are accounts of drinking, bed-hopping and general partying. Also among the luminaries was Aldous Huxley. Down the pass at the Pen-y-Gwryd Hotel, it was the later climbing stars of the 1950s who frequented this base for training, with the aim to climb Everest and also Kangchenjunga. The Alpine-hut feeling of the places adds to its unmistakable and somewhat reverential ambience. On the walls are signed photographs of the legends and items from the successful 1953 expedition and many more after.

Y Lliwedd to Snowdon

You'll dip down again until reaching the junction with the Watkin Path at **C** 🔄 **SH619536** where there is a large cairn. The Watkin Path is another little-used path to the summit, mainly because it starts at the lowest elevation of all the routes. It is named after Edward Watkin, an MP and railway owner who attempted to dig a Channel tunnel in the 1880s. He had a summer home near the beginning of the path.

Below this col is Glaslyn, the lake into which Sir Bedivere threw King Arthur's sword Excalibur, according to Welsh Folklore. It was also believed to be bottomless, but in fact is around 39 metres deep. From the col and junction with the Watkin Path there's a clear but steep zigzagging path up the left of the ridge line. An ice axe and crampons would be required here if there's snow on the ground, but otherwise it's fairly solid. A head for heights will always be useful, but you probably haven't got this far without one! It is along this ridge, Bwlch y Saethau (the Pass of the Arrows), where King Arthur is said to have died.

Our path climbs up to reach the Rhyd Ddu Path that comes up from the village of the same name. A large standing stone marks the junction at **D** 🔄 **SH608542**. Turn right for the last couple of hundred metres to the summit of Snowdon, known as Yr Wyddfa, and some of the country's most spectacular views… although the large cafe is somewhat of a distraction. After the route up, it's also usually a little surprising to see so many people. On clear days, Northern Ireland, the Republic of Ireland, England and Scotland are all visible, and apparently 24 counties.

Like so many early summits, it was a botanist who first recorded the climb to Snowdon's peak. Thomas Johnson, a Royalist colonel in the English Civil War and known as the 'father of British field botany', climbed the mountain in 1639, although it was almost certainly climbed earlier. The summit visitor centre, Hafod Eryri, is an award-winning construction at the top of Snowdon. There has been some kind of building on the summit since at least 1820 and the current building, opened in 2009, stands in contrast to its predecessor which was memorably described by Prince Charles as the "highest slum in Wales". It was in 1896 that the Snowdon Mountain Railway arrived, and with it hundreds of people. Today, more than 130,000 passengers a year use the train to reach Snowdon's summit.

SNOWDON FOLKLORE

There's a rich folklore surrounding Snowdon mountain. According to legend, the summit itself is the tomb of Rhitta Gawr, a giant who lived in Snowdonia. He overcame the armies of 26 English kings making a cape out of the kings' beards. The arrogant Rhitta Gawr also demanded the beard of King Arthur, but at a fight in Snowdonia, Rhitta was slain by Arthur. A cairn or tumulus was built over his body called Gwyddfa Rhudda (Rhita's Cairn) and over the centuries this became Yr Wyddfa or Snowdon.

Arthurian legend also relates that the ridge between Y Lliwedd and Snowdon called Bwlch y Saethau, where our walk takes us, is where Arthur died. Below this ridge, Glaslyn tarn is where he asked Sir Bedivere to throw Excalibur. Arthur's body was brought to this lake from where it was carried to Afallon and his men hid in caves in Y Lliwedd where they remain until they are needed again. On the opposite side of Glaslyn is Crib-y-Ddygsl, under which is our return path, where Merlin hid the golden throne of Britain from the Saxons. It's never been found.

Legends hang thick in the air around Snowdon

View south-west from Y Lliwedd

Snowdon to Pen-y-Pass car park

From the summit, walk along the path to Bwlch Glas at **E** (☉) SH607548 (beware of cornices in winter) and the top of the Pyg Track where there is a standing stone. The steep cliffs down below to the left, called Clogwyn Du'r Arddu, hold some of the best climbing in the country. Some of the most influential climbers, such as Joe Brown and Don Whillans, cut their teeth on these slopes. Remarkably, the cliffs were first climbed in 1798 by, yes, a couple of botanists looking for plants. What they were likely looking for would include the famous Snowdon lily, an Alpine plant first discovered by Edward Lhuyd in the 1690s. The lily has been here since the last ice age, but it is thought that only 100 plants remain – it is dying out

because of climate change. The wonderfully colourful Snowdon beetle can also be found up here, as can Peregrine falcons and wheatears.

The top of the Pyg Track is a bit of a steep drop down at first, and if there's any doubt, then it is best to take the Llanberis Path back down into Llanberis and grab a cab or bus back up to Pen-y-Pass car park. If it is icy or snowy then do this regardless. The Pyg Track is described by the National Park Authority as 'the most rugged and challenging of the six paths up to Snowdon' (the Y Lliwedd route isn't an official route up).

The origin of the name Pyg Track is a mystery. Theories include that is was the route up from the Pen y Gwryd Hotel; that it is named for Bwlch y Moch (Pigs' Gap), through which it passes; or that the track was used to carry 'pyg' (black tar) up to the copper mines. Whatever, it's now a long

Tyn y Coed inn

Pen-y-Gwryd Hotel

descent down the path that clings to the mountainside under Crib-y-Ddysgl and the knife-edge arête that is Crib Goch.

Above Glaslyn lake the path forks at a standing stone where the Miners' Track and Pyg Track meet. Stay left to follow the Pyg Track. By Glaslyn below you'll see the remains of a copper mine. Keep descending along the path. At Bwlch y Moch you'll see a fork that leads up to Crib Goch. Continue descending now back down to Pen-y-Pass car park and then on for a well-deserved pint.

There are several beer options nearby, although none listed in the *Good Beer Guide*. YHA Snowdon Pen-y-Pass across the road serves beer – and this hotel itself has remarkable Everest connections – but, perhaps the most atmospheric place in

the area is the **1 Pen-y-Gwryd Hotel** located at the bottom of Pen-y-Pass as it meets the A498 at the head of the Nant Gwynant valley. It is from here that Edmund Hillary and Tenzing Norgay, along with expedition leader John Hunt, trained for their successful 1953 ascent of the world's highest mountain. This hotel, along with what is now YHA Snowdon Pen-y-Pass, had long been at the centre of British climbing, right through the golden age. Today, in this former farmhouse, memorabilia from that historic climb can be perused as you sup on a pint. It is a place that exudes history. If you would like to spend longer here, there are also rooms available.

Another great beer option is at **2 Plas y Brenin**, the National Mountain Centre on the way into Capel Curig. As well as providing a multitude of courses (several of which this author has done), there is an excellent bar that features beer from local breweries, many of them very small. Purple Moose and the Brenin's own beer were available on our visit. It's a pleasant, modern bar that serves meals and provides fantastic views over Snowdon.

Finally, on the other side of Capel Curig is the **3 Tyn-y-Coed Inn**, marked by a stagecoach outside. There is a spacious bar here, with an open fire and handpumps featuring ales from Purple Moose and Black Sheep on our visit. A number of comfortable rooms are also available.

PUB INFORMATION

1 Pen-y-Gwryd Hotel
Nant Gwynant, Gwynedd, LL55 4NT
01286 870211 • pyg.co.uk •
Opening hours: call for details

2 Plas y Brenin
Capel Curig, LL24 0ET
01690 720214 • pyb.co.uk
Opening hours: 12-2, 5-11 Mon-Fri; 12-11 Sat & Sun

3 Tyn-y-Coed Inn
Capel Curig, LL24 0EE •
01690 720331 • tyn-y-coed.co.uk
Opening hours: 3-11 Mon-Thur; 12-11 Fri-Sun

Glyderau

There are few walks anywhere that match this: the grandeur of scenery, the thrill of vertiginous passes, the otherworldly geological jumble and one of the country's most loved mountains. This is the Glyderau, a mountain group in North Wales just north-east of Snowdon, and it offers one of the best mountain days out anywhere. If the magnificent naughty twins of Glyder Fawr and Glyder Fach weren't enough, there's an optional extra: a scramble up the shark's fin of Tryfan. And that's all before we touch upon the significance of Darwin's geological discoveries while walking in this area.

▸ **Start/finish:** Car park at Idwal Cottage

▸ **Duration:** 3.5–5hrs

▸ **Distance:** 6 miles (9.5km)

▸ **Ascent:** 2,696ft (822m)

▸ **Fitness:**

▸ **Navigation:**

▸ **OS map:** Explorer OL17 *Snowdon/Yr Wyddfa*

▸ **Key attractions:** Zipworld, Bounce Below, Snowdon Mountain Railway

▸ **THE PUBS:** Sior, Douglas Arms Hotel, both Bethesda

▸ **Timing tip:** If you are climbing Tryfan be sure to add at least an hour

A spiky rock outcrop on Glyder Fach

The northern shoreline of Llyn Idwal

This is a walk that requires some composure – there's a satisfying walk up through the sharp Devil's Kitchen that, although steep, isn't quite classed as a scramble, and some careful navigation in poor weather is needed. Our route also heads past the southern ridge of Tryfan. While we don't describe a route up (or down!), few experienced hillwalkers or scramblers would be able to resist its magnetic pull. For the post-walk pint, it's a couple of miles to the lively town of Bethesda for a choice of pubs including two regulars from the *Good Beer Guide*.

Climbing up through the Devil's Kitchen

Idwal Cottage to Glyder Fawr

There's a car park at Idwal Cottage by the fairly new visitor centre that while handy is often full so, arrive early. There are a couple of other car parks alongside Llyn Ogwen, but they're not ideal. This is a very popular spot when the sun is out.

From the visitor centre (worth a scout around on your return), walk past the Darwin wall and through the gates, resisting the urge to go through the gully. Climb out along the path south-east and take the first path off to the right towards Llyn Idwal. The path rises gently to the lake that marks Cwm Idwal, a perfect example of a hanging valley (a tributary valley higher than the main valley). Cwm means cirque, a half-open steep-sided hollow at the head of a valley.

As you draw up to the lake it's impossible not to be taken aback by the drama of the place as Snowdonia's giants rise up about you. It was once voted one of Britain's great natural wonders. It certainly impressed Charles Darwin (see box) who, while standing not far from where you are in the 1840s, theorised that what he was standing in was in actual fact a valley scooped out by vast glaciers. It was the first time anyone had posited that glaciers once covered the UK. The geological

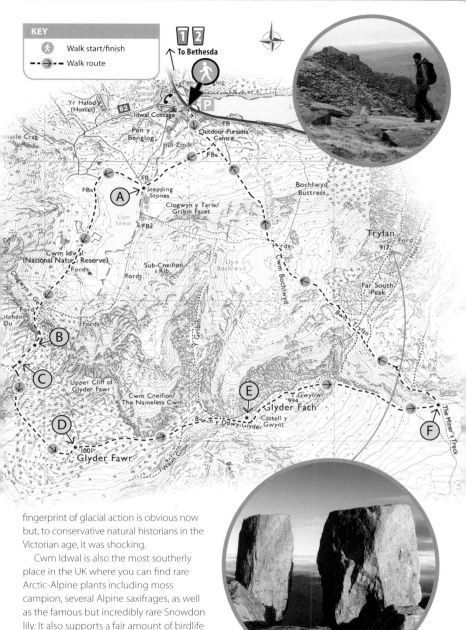

KEY

👤 Walk start/finish

-- ▷ -- Walk route

1 2
↑ **To Bethesda**

fingerprint of glacial action is obvious now but, to conservative natural historians in the Victorian age, it was shocking.

Cwm Idwal is also the most southerly place in the UK where you can find rare Arctic-Alpine plants including moss campion, several Alpine saxifrages, as well as the famous but incredibly rare Snowdon lily. It also supports a fair amount of birdlife such as ring ouzels, wheatears, ravens and Peregrine falcons. However, do you see any flying over the lake? According to Welsh folklore, Llyn Idwal is the last resting place of

Adam & Eve on top of Tryfan

153

A short scramble on the Devil's Kitchen

Prince Idwal Foel, one of the ancient princes of Gwynedd, who drowned here. No birds fly over the lake as a result.

At the junction in front of the lake at **A** SH646598, turn right along the shoreline and follow the clear path around the west side and towards the back of Cwm Idwal. In fact, there's no great difference whichever way you go around the lake. If you go around the east side it gives you a chance to look more closely at the Idwal Slabs, a well-known beginners' climbing wall.

As you head south, you'll start to make out the path that leads up through the Devil's Kitchen. It seems quite daunting, but it's actually fine when you approach it, with a pretty clear path. However, there is usually water everywhere so, care is needed and you'll be pleased of a pair of leather boots. As the path starts to steepen, try to work out its direction well in advance. There are places where the path is unclear as it crosses bedrock but, you should pick it up easily enough. There may be a couple of places where you'll need to put a hand down, but it's not too much of a scramble and given the amount of water around it can also be

a bit slippery in places. Some new walkers hesitate a bit at the drop, but you'd have to go pretty wrong for anything to happen.

Continue climbing up to and above the large buttress. Towards the top of the Devil's Kitchen is a wall and a stile around **B** SH639586. Be sure to drink in the excellent views from here!

Climb over the stile and up the wide rocky path. Stay to the right; we're looking for a path that rises up to the south-east to Glyder Fawr. The path starts splitting off at **C** SH638585 and above you, around the back of a prominent buttress, you should be able to see the route leading up some scree. If you've arrived at Llyn y Cwn, you've gone a little too far. The path starts off up the scree, but as it begins to flatten out, there are some large cairns that lead you towards the summit.

In fog, you'll definitely need to be following your compass – get a rough direction towards the summit at **D** SH642579. It's a rough direction because the best path doesn't head directly to the summit. As you'll see on approaching it, the top of Glyder Fawr, standing at 1,001 metres, is a chaotic crash of shattered rocks, split boulders and scree. The geological pressure on the Glyders seems raw and recent,

Shattered rocks on Glyder Fach

The enticing Tryfan is a proper hands-on mountain

its jagged piles unlike other summits in Snowdonia. The word Glyder is said to derive from the Welsh word Gludair that means 'heap of stones', although on seeing the summit this seems to have a been given with a certain understatement.

The path to the summit leads south-west with the final approach west. It's a mess up here and even the summit itself is a group of sharp rocks stood to attention – don't expect a cairn, trig point or shelter.

Glyder Fawr to Bwlch Tryfan

Once you've located the summit, thankfully the path on the other side is a little clearer and certainly flatter. There are some cairns leading the way, but in fog, it's tricky to make them out from all the other rocks and boulders. A subtle path heads east around the top of Cwm Cneifion (the Nameless

DARWIN'S IDWAL

Charles Darwin first travelled to Cwm Idwal in 1831, when he was intrigued by the many large boulders which had seemingly been dropped and shattered and which, he noticed, contained marine seashells. He wondered whether they were once formed within an ancient ocean. It was after a later visit, however, that Darwin developed a further, more controversial theory about the cwm. He realised that the hanging valley of Cwm Idwal must, in fact, have been riven by a vast glacier and that such geological processes would occur very slowly over vast periods of time, making the world much older than most interpretations of its age in the Bible. Along with his theory on the origins of species, Darwin's views caused huge controversy in Victorian society.

If you look around the cwm today, the large mounds up toward Tryfan are moraines (glacial deposits) that we now know were left by retreating glaciers more than 11,000 years ago.

Cwm Clyd; a classic glaciated hanging valley on the western side of Cwm Idwal

Cwm). Again, take a compass bearing in fog. After you pass the top of Y Gribin, a popular scramble up, there are a couple of paths that pass along Bwlch y Ddwy-Glyder above the cwm on the other side of Y Gribin. We took the higher path so we could poke our nose over the precipitous drop. The route up to Glyder Fach at 994 metres is also a jumble and requires picking your way through the ankle-eating boulders. The path up, as marked on the OS map, skirts south around the 972-metre rocky outcrop at **E** ⊕ SH654582 known as Castell y Gwynt, but few can resist its pull. It's often confused with the summit when approaching from the west; instead, it is classed as a top of Glyder Fach. This feature, along with the Cantilever Stone that we'll find soon, was depicted in Walt Disney's *Dragonslayer*. Our route climbs up to this famous feature

Monolith on Glyder Fach

and then follows a clear path across to the summit boulders of Glyder Fach along the top of the cliffs. There's a scramble to the top of the boulders if you want to get to the high point. Just behind it is the famous Cantilever Stone, a long, thin, horizontal boulder that appears unbalanced – it's almost obligatory to climb onto it for a photo!

From up here, Tryfan seems attractively spiky – a floozie of a mountain. From the summit of Glyder Fach, we head down to the east. There is a more direct route down to the col between Glyder Fach and Tryfan, known as Bwlch Tryfan, but frankly it's a slightly terrifying stumble down some horrible scree. It's easier to climb up than down but, either way, it's unpleasant. Instead, head to the top of Bristly Ridge, a well-known scramble up from the col, and then climb over east to follow a path down.

It's important not to head at all down to the north here, but continue to the south of the cliff edge. You'll have to pick your way down over some shattered boulders at first before the path is clearly seen. You'll see Y Foel Goch ahead of you and down at the col and a small tarn marked as Llyn Caseg-friath on the map. 100 metres before the llyn, is a crossroads at ⓕ 🕒 SH667583. It's also important not to be tempted down earlier than this point. Once you get there, however, you'll see the track skirt back down north-west below the cliff. If it's clear you should be able to trace it down all the way to the col Bwlch Tryfan. There are a couple of steep bits that can also be slippery, so care is needed, but otherwise it's a good path and offers amazing views of Tryfan. Ignore any of the other paths shooting off to the right. It descends a little lower than the col and requires a bit of a pull back up to the wall and stile under Tryfan.

The stile at Bwlch Tryfan

Bwlch Tryfan to Idwal Cottage

Tryfan is one of the country's best mountains, thanks largely to its pleasing pointy peak. It's also the only mountain in Wales that can't be climbed without the use of hands. But it's also a great place for a spot of scrambling. A common ascent for a day out scrambling is up to the north ridge, a Grade 1 ascent up the easiest line, down to the col and then up Bristly Ridge. Many people use ropes and helmets during the ascent.

We're stood under the south ridge, which is also a Grade 1 scramble, but without too much exposure except in a couple of places. The route up is complicated and beyond the remit of this book to describe in detail, but there are plenty of guides online. It is mostly a matter using your experience to pick a line up to the summit, either over the Far South Peak or, as an easier option, around this and along the route marked on the OS map. Once on the top, there are two monoliths known as Adam (on the left) and Eve (on the right). There's a challenge to jump from one to the other, which doesn't seem too bad until you get under them and see the drop to the east!

Looking down the Ogwen Valley towards Bethesda

Welsh ales at the Douglas Arms

A welcoming fire in the Sior

If you're climbing Tryfan, on the return you can weave your way down to the path above Llyn Bochlwyd rather than return to the stile at the col Bwlch Tryfan.

Otherwise, from the col, cross the stile over the wall and take the clear path down, quite steeply at first towards Llyn Bochlwyd. It's boggy down by the lake, and tricky to pick out the path. Cross the top of Nant Bochlwyd just below the outlet and above the drop to pick up a path on the other side. Take care on the slippery rocks. The path then weaves down, quite steeply in places, to the left of Nant Bochlwyd. If you think your walk is nearly over, beware it can get a bit strenuous. If there's ice on the ground it is treacherous. Finally, it does begin to flatten out as it reaches the junction of the path we took at the beginning of the day to Llyn Idwal. It's then a short drop back to the car

park. The visitor centre is worth a look, but by now the pint will be calling.

It's a short hop, not more than 10 minutes, into Bethesda, the nearest village. It's a lively and friendly little place with a quarrying heritage. There is no shortage of pubs in the town and it is lucky enough to have two regular entries in the *Good Beer Guide*. The **Douglas Arms Hotel** is also listed as a CAMRA Real Heritage Pub with an interior of special historical interest and is known for its full-sized snooker table. The sharp-eyed will notice that there is also an orange and a purple ball on the table, for a game known as snooker plus. The building itself is a coaching inn dating back to the 1820s, and the four public rooms are little changed since the 1930s. It is thought to be the last pub in the country to convert to decimal currency. As well as three handpumps dispensing cask beers there's also a good selection of whiskies.

The **Sior** (aka the George) is in Carneddi, a minute or two above Bethesda High Street, and very much worth the trip up. This is a fantastic little pub, with a great selection of beers, a log fire and friendly staff and locals. We enjoyed it here! On our visit there were beers from Heavy Industry and Big Bog among others – there's an ever-changing selection. This is the pub to visit after a long, fun day on the mountains.

PUB INFORMATION

Douglas Arms Hotel
High Street, Bethesda, LL57 3AY
01248 600219 • douglasarmsbethesda.co.uk
Opening hours: 6-11 Mon-Thu; 3.30-midnight Sat; 1-3, 7-11 Sun

Sior (George)
35-37 Carneddi Road, Bethesda, LL57 3SE
01248 600072
Opening hours: 7-midnight Mon-Thu; 5-1am Fri; 1-1am Sat; 1-midnight Sun

Talybont to Brecon via Pen y Fan

WALK

20

The central Brecon Beacons rise steeply from the south coast of Wales before falling dramatically towards the town of Brecon. This long and arduous walk takes in all the six main Old Red Sandstone peaks, including the 886-metre (2,907-foot) Pen y Fan, the highest peak in all of southern Britain. Yet the thrill of the vertiginous drops and vast views across southern Wales more than make up for it, as do the excellent pubs in the area. There is no doubt that it is a tough walk and some of the navigation, especially at the start, can be challenging. The weather is also liable to change at any time so you need to be prepared in full mountain gear.

> **Start:** Talybont-on-Usk

> **Finish:** Brecon

> **Access:** No. 43 bus to Talybont-on-Usk from Brecon (6 a day; not Sunday)

> **Duration:** 6.5–8hrs

> **Distance:** 15 miles (24km)

> **Ascent:** 3,789ft (1,155m)

> **Fitness:**

> **Navigation:**

> **OS map:** Explorer OL12 Brecon Beacons National Park (Western Area)

> **Key attractions:** Pen y Fan, the highest mountain in southern Britain; Brecon Castle

> **THE PUBS:** Star Inn, Talybont-on-Usk; Brecon Castle Hotel, Boar's Head, Brecon Tap, Clarence, all Brecon. Try also: White Hart, Talybont-on-Usk

> **Timing tips:** This walk can be walked in reverse, finishing with two atmospheric pubs in Talybont-on-Usk. It can also be cut shortened by 5km by descending west along the Beacons Way from Pen y Fan to the car park on the A470 and taking a bus to Brecon. Given the remote nature of these towns it's important to check transport timings – note there are no buses to Talybont-on-Usk on Sundays

Talybont Reservoir as seen from along the causeway

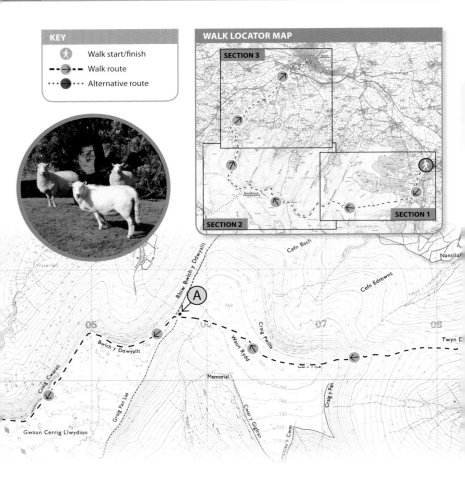

There's little to suggest the majesty, and quite frankly, difficulty of this walk when you arrive in the amiable little village of Talybont-on-Usk. It's little more than a handful of houses, yet manages to support three pubs, one of them, the **1 Star Inn**, is good enough for an entry in the *Good Beer Guide* and to win the Brecknock Pub of the Year seven years in a row. The large beer garden sits next to the Monmouthshire & Brecon Canal, but it's the ever-changing selection of beer and local cider that is the highlight. There were nine pumps on when we visited, and the huge array of pump clips around the

wall is testament to the range of local and national real ales on offer. It's almost worth doing this walk backwards just to end up here, but that would mean the grand finale of Pen y Fan would come first. Either way, try to fashion a trip back here. Also worth visiting is the **6 White Hart**. It's a genuine community pub despite being on the Taff Trail, and popular with walkers and those puttering along the canal. There's an interesting selection of naval paraphernalia and a little seating area under what seems like a knocked through fireplace. It's a nice pub despite a preponderance of signs telling you what to, or not, to do.

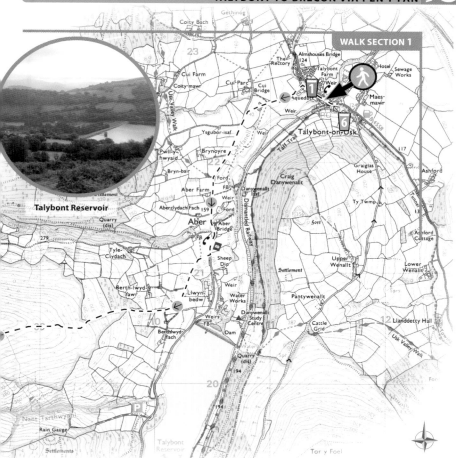

WALK SECTION 1

Enough talking about pubs; first there's a very big hill ahead of you that needs to be attacked. It is, frankly, a cruel start to the walk but one that will reward you a hundredfold later in the day. So, take a deep breath and walk from the Star Inn north and take the first left that rises briskly to a canal bridge. The Monmouthshire & Brecon Canal is now a 56-kilometre (35-mile) canal. It was once two different canals that were part of a network in South Wales built in the final years of the 18th century to carry coal and iron. They were both left to run in 1962, but part of the Monmouthshire & Brecon Canal was reopened for leisure use in 1970. There are plans to open up more of the network.

Looking back over to YHA Brecon Beacons Danywenallt

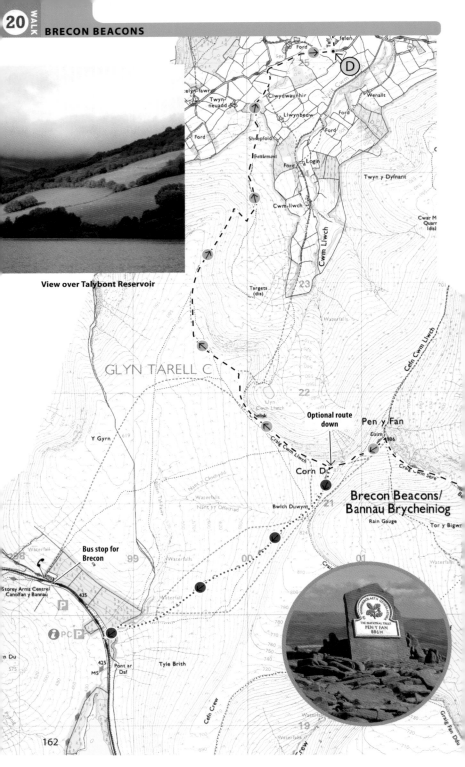

View over Talybont Reservoir

GLYN TARELL C

Optional route down

Pen y Fan

Corn Du

Brecon Beacons/
Bannau Brycheiniog

Rain Gauge

Bus stop for Brecon

Storey Arms Centre/
Canolfan y Bannau

Pont ar Daf

Tyle Brith

View of Pen y Fan from Fan y Big

first destination of the (very) long day.

Continue along this rocky path, ignoring the bridleway sign on the right. It soon opens into a slightly flatter boggy area, but continue following the path roughly west (it's far from a straight path) and continue climbing this exhausting start. But don't forget to turn around. The views to the east are over the Black Mountains, a range that spreads east into Herefordshire in England and north to Hay-on-Wye. Walk 21 explores some of the highest peaks in this area. Also, the Black Mountains are not to be confused with the Black Mountain which is a range that rises to the west of the Brecon Beacons National Park between Camarthenshire and Powys. To make matters even more confusing, one of the highest peaks in the Black Mountains (plural!) is called, yep, you guess it, the Black Mountain. If nothing else, figuring it out will take your mind off the lung-busting ascent. Also, more immediately south is Talybont Reservoir, a great body of water

Over the bridge, continue along the lane to the T-junction. It's a quiet road, but there is no pavement. A footpath runs parallel to the road along the waterway running from Talybont Reservoir. Turn left at the junction and meander through the village of Aber, about a kilometre away. Cross Aber Bridge and take the second lane right following until it turns into a footpath. Keep an eye out on the left for a fingerpost that reads 'Twyn Du', the

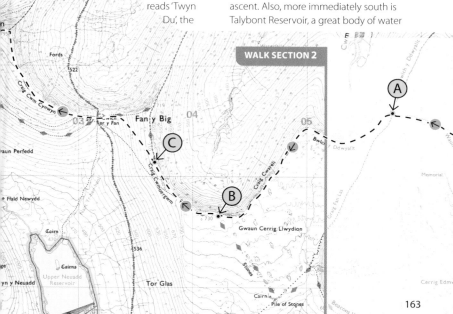

Across the Beacons from Fan y Big

that is a popular site for birdwatching and trout fishing. Cross the causeway and it will lead to the delightful YHA Brecon Beacons Danywenallt. It's a converted farmhouse and has several private rooms, as well as dorm and camping areas. It's a good alternative to start this walk too.

The path levels off briefly at a cairn, and in good weather you'll be able to see the daunting path ahead of you that zigzags up Craig y Fan. Weave your way up to the summit cairn and get your bearings,

literally – this part can be a challenge in mist. You're heading for the crossing of paths at Ⓐ ⊕ SO057204, where there are steep drops either side of this narrow ridge. At the col, there are two marked paths heading west, the northernmost one sweeps around Bwlch y Ddwyallt, as marked on the 1:25,000 map, and along Craig Cwareli to the next peak of Fan y Big. You want to be taking the path that heads west along the ridge with the drop on your right. In fact, from now on the walk generally follows an extremely steep, almost cliff-like drop, generally, but not always, on the northern

aspect of the mountain. Take great care, it's a trip you do not want to be taking. The edge of Craig Cwareli is a case in point, dropping 200 metres almost vertically down into the valley below. That said, there is a clear path that skirts the drop all the way to Corn Du.

The vertiginously-sided mountain range, known as the central Beacons has an aspect unlike any other in the country. The Old Red Sandstone, laid down in the Devonian period, descends gently south to the South Wales Coalfield basin, but the deep northern aspects of the mountains were carved out by glaciers that formed on the leeward side of the high ground. You'll generally notice that the southwesterly winds blow the clouds over and down these deep drops. It's a particular problem in winter when dangerous cornices can form.

Looking down to Cwm Llwch from Pen Milan

The path, once you're on the right one, is mostly easy to follow from now on. You'll know you're on it, because there's a huge drop off to your right only a metre or so away. Take care on the rocky paths, and follow the path around the vast Cwm Oergwn. At **B** SO041197, we now start an on-off fling with the Beacons Way, a 152-kilometre (95-mile) walk across

165

the entire Brecon Beacons National Park between Abergavenny in the east and Llangadog in the west.

At **C** ⏱ **SO036201**, the path forks. An indistinct jumble of rocks and tussock leads up to the summit cairn of Fan y Big for the keen. In bad weather it's easier to descend on the clear path NNW to the col known as Bwlch ar y Fan. Here an ancient trail, known as the Gap Road, crosses the mountain ridge that is a bridleway popular with mountain bikers. At the col, you'll often find other walkers grabbing a snack before the steep-looking climb up to Cribyn. A National Trust sign here announces Craig Cwm Cynwyn. The Beacons Way traverses Cribyn, but we're going up that steep path to the commanding 795-metre outpost that affords huge views over the entire area, including north to the Cambrian Mountains.

Wye Valley beer on the terrace at the Brecon Castle Hotel

As well as views over the mountains, this part of the Brecon Beacons is also home to birds of prey including peregrine falcons, buzzards and the red kite, easily identifiable by their forked tail. Ravens too can be seen.

From the summit of Cribyn, we sweep back down west along a steep path (slippery when wet – which it will be!), rejoin the Beacons Way at the col, and struggle back up to our highest point of the day and the highest point in southern Britain: Pen y Fan at 2907ft (886 metres), only 199 metres lower than Snowdon.

From the summit of Pen y Fan on a clear day, you can see the Bristol Channel, Swansea Bay, the Gower Peninsula, the Cambrian Mountains and into England and Shropshire's Clee Hills. Seemingly in all weathers there are people bagging this peak, and seemingly there are always a couple of

The route back along Pen Milan towards Corn Du

people in utterly inappropriate clothing and footwear too, heading to touch the summit cairn that has been there since the Bronze Age. There is also a cist on the summit, which is a box made from straight stone slabs that would have once held the remains of a long-deceased Bronze Age ancestor.

Some souls brave the narrow ridge down north along Cefn Cwm Llwch, but we're going to sweep around to the anvil-shaped Corn Du, the final peak of the day. It's yet another steep descent and brisk ascent back to the 2,864-foot (873-metre) summit but, bear in mind, once there, it's all downhill from now on. Corn Du also has a Bronze Age cairn and burial cist.

Here you can make a choice between short walk down west along the Beacons Way to the A470, or the long walk into Brecon itself. We'll describe the latter but, if you take the shorter option, there are somewhat sporadic buses into Brecon along the A470 from the Storey Arms (don't get excited, it's not a pub anymore!).

If you are walking into Brecon from Corn Du, follow the path Craig Cwm Llwch. It can be tricky to find the route in low cloud, but a little climb down west from the summit and it becomes clear. Do not climb down north, it's just a very steep drop. Be sure to follow a compass here.

That said, once you've found the path – which should be easy to see in good weather – continue descending north-west. You'll pass a little obelisk that was erected for Tommy Jones, a five-year-old boy who died around here in the summer of 1900. Tommy went missing on an errand down in the valley and his remains were eventually found at this spot after capturing the imagination of the entire nation. It's still a mystery how this little boy, who died of exhaustion and exposure, could have climbed the 400 metres and two miles from the place he was last seen. The obelisk has an inscription that reads: "This obelisk marks the spot where the body of Tommy Jones aged 5 was found. He lost his way between Cwm Llwch Farm and the Login on the night of August 4th 1900.

The Brecon Castle Hotel

After an anxious search of 29 days his body was found on September 2nd.".

From the obelisk, continue down the ridge to the to the fields at the bottom. An indistinct path leads to a gate at the bottom (keep an eye on your compass here), through a pleasant wooded track over stream and onto the lane. We now hit the Taff Trail heading east for half a kilometre along the road. At **D** 🕐 SO007251 follow the fingerpost marked Taff Trail north through farming fields. You'll come across a gorgeous little waterfall by a house. Skirt around the building to the right and you'll emerge onto a narrow road. The Taff Trail continues along this quiet lane all the way into the centre of Brecon where a pint awaits; and trust us, you'll need it after this walk. After going under the A40 bridge, turn right at the T-junction and walk into the centre over the River Usk.

Brecon is a lovely little town, with the ruins of a romantic castle nestled in its centre. The town was first built in 1093 by the Norman Lord Bernard de Neufmarche. The motte-and-bailey castle was the first stone castle in Wales. Today, the site is home to the **2** **Brecon Castle Hotel**, which has a decent bar which was serving beer from

Inside the Brecon Tap (left & right)

the Wye Valley Brewery, including their golden Butty Bach that is popular in these parts. Although the interior feels like a hotel restaurant bar (which it is) the views from the terrace over the mountains you've just climbed are excellent. Another good pub with a wide selection of cask ales and other craft beers is the riverside free house, the **3 Boar's Head**.

A new find in town is the **4 Brecon Tap**, a lovely bar opened by Brecon Brewing. It's pleasingly wooden, with hops hanging from the ceiling. On entering, there's a wide selection of bottled beers from small breweries across Wales, including Tiny Rebel and Otley. On the pumps are Brecon Brewing's own cask beers, plus a couple of guests ales. There are also other craft beers

from around the world along with local cider. Although it only opened in March 2016, the Tap is already a popular place thanks to its excellent beer selection and friendly staff. It feels like the kind of place where you can put your feet up (after taking your muddy boots off) and spend the afternoon relaxing with a newspaper.

Another good pub option in Brecon is the **5 Clarence**, a lively pub that has a couple of guest beers on offer alongside the regulars, usually from Wye Valley Brewery. There are a couple of well-used dart boards and a pleasant beer garden. There's a real sense of community around this pub. You might want to settle in for a while until it's time to jump back the bus back to Talybont and the Star Inn.

PUB INFORMATION

1 STAR INN
Talybont-on-Usk, LD3 7YX
01874 676635 • starinntalybont.co.uk • 🛏
Opening hours: 5-11 Mon-Fri; 12-11 Sat & Sun

2 BRECON CASTLE HOTEL
Castle Square, Brecon, LD3 9DB
01874 624611 • breconcastle.co.uk • 🛏
Opening hours: 11-11

3 BOAR'S HEAD
Ship Street, Brecon, LD3 9AD
01874 622856 • facebook.com/boarsbrecon
Opening hours: 12-midnight (1am Thu; 1.30am Fri & Sat); closed Sun

4 BRECON TAP
6 Bullwark, Brecon, LD3 7LB
01874 623888 • facebook.com/brecontap
Opening hours: 11-11 (midnight Fri & Sat)

5 CLARENCE
25 The Watton, Brecon, LD3 7ED
01874 622810 • clarenceinn.co.uk • 🛏
Opening hours: 12-midnight (2am Fri & Sat)

Try also:

6 WHITE HART
Talybont-on-Usk, LD3 7JD
01874 676227 • whitehartinntalybont.co.uk • 🛏
Opening hours: 11-11 Sun-Thu; 11-11.30 Fri & Sat

Crickhowell Circular

WALK
21

It's not hard to see how the Black Mountains got their name: as the sun hides behind the cloud (as it does a fair bit in these parts), the lumbering hills of the area darken with dramatic effect. Yet when the sun does appear, no matter what the season, they are an inviting prospect for a hillwalker. The Black Mountains lie in the eastern area of the Brecon Beacons National Park and, while they don't hold the magnetic draw of Pen y Fan in the east, these little-visited mountains offer a walk of solitude and probably the most magnificent views across southern Wales from anywhere, including from its more famous neighbours. This walk from the lovely town of Crickhowell takes in ancient burial sites, remote mountain passes and, of course, some delightful pubs full of history (and good beer).

▶ **Start/finish:** Bear Hotel, Crickhowell

▶ **Access:** Regular buses from Brecon and Abergavenny (43 & X43)

▶ **Duration:** 5–7hrs

▶ **Distance:** 11.8 miles (19km)

▶ **Ascent:** 2,627ft (801m)

▶ **Fitness:**

▶ **Navigation:**

▶ **OS map:** Explorer OL13 *Brecon Beacons National Park (Eastern Area)*

▶ **Key attractions:** Table Mountain, Crickhowell, Crickhowell Castle

▶ **THE PUBS:** Bear Hotel, Crickhowell; Red Lion, Llanbedr. Try also: Bridge End Inn, Crickhowell

▶ **Timing tip:** There is a long walk out from Llanbedr that could be shortened by taking a taxi or getting a lift

Looking up the ridge path to Pen Cerrig-calch

Wild pony on Pen Allt-mawr

Crickhowell is a delightfully tidy town. Bunting often hangs across the streets, the tourist information centre sells local jams and carved wooden love spoons, and a literary festival takes over the town at the beginning of October. It's rightly popular with tourists, but not so much with walkers who, understandably, head farther west to highest mountain in the area: Pen y Fan (see Walk 20). Yet, the 719-metre (2,360-foot) bulk of Pen Allt-mawr, the third highest peak in the Black Mountains, is just as impressive as the some of the western mountains, but very few people visit it; you're unlikely to see too many people on this walk. It's made all the more appealing given it takes in a large Iron-Age Celtic hill fort, known as Table Mountain for obvious reasons

Old carved sideboard in the Bear Hotel

as you'll see, with the earthworks still clearly visible, and wide open views that take in a 360-degree panorama of the mountains of the area. The Sugar Loaf, Pen y Fan and the nearby Llangattock Escarpment can all be seen in the south and east, while farther north the views up into mid-Wales are equally striking.

The old conundrum of where to park on a hill walk is particularly apt here, and, frankly the higher you go, the less you'll have to walk. However, for the sake of public transport users we'll start in the easily accessible town centre of Crickhowell. If you are a motorist, follow the route and park as high up as you like.

From the Bear Hotel (which we'll visit later), walk along the A40 westwards, past the petrol station and right on to Llanbedr Road. There's good parking in the road parallel to this. Walk up this road and through where the trees close in. Be careful here as there's no pavement. As it meets Great Oak Road, turn left briefly along the road, again taking care of the cars. When the road bends around to the right you'll see a small track straight ahead, which you'll need to take, ignoring the footpath that heads west. Go through the gate directly north to a farm marked 'The Wern'. You'll see Table Mountain ahead of you; the first destination of the day. At the houses, follow a footpath sign east

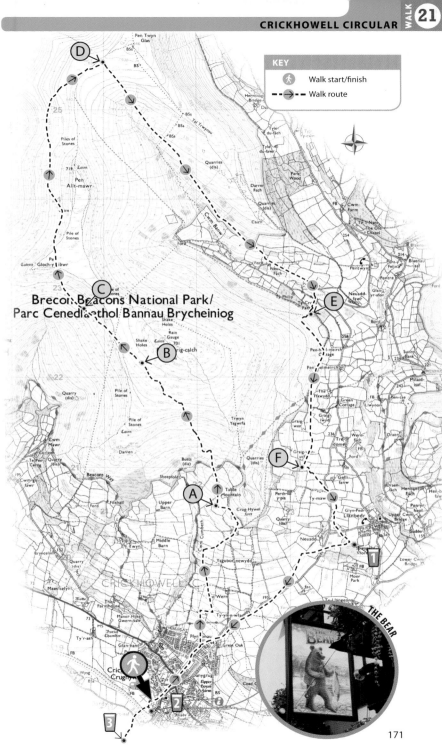

The Bear Hotel

valleys beyond, while over to the west Pen y Fan, the highest mountain of the Brecon Beacons, should come into view, towering above the lesser peaks before it.

Follow the hand-painted sign to the right for a short, but pleasant stretch through some thick woodland. The path opens up and weaves through the bracken around the south east of Table Mountain. Keep left at the first fork, and follow that path until you reach a three-way fork. Take the left hand path that leads directly to the top of Table Mountain **A** 🕐 SO225206, or Crug Hywel to give it its ancient Welsh name and that which gives its name to the town of Crickhowell. It's easy to see why ancient Celts chose this pleasingly rounded spur of Pen Cerrig-calch for a fort; it's uniquely placed with a 360-degree view of the surrounding area. Like many of the mountains in the Brecon Beacons, the steep sided aspects of the mountains were thought to be caused by large landslips after the last ice age when the weaker strata below gave way under the weight of the heavier strata above them.

The old ramparts and a stone ditch can clearly be seen on the top of Table Mountain, especially from the side. The views from here are glorious. If you're tight on time, Table Mountain makes a great destination to take a flask of tea in the morning before heading back to Crickhowell. We're going onward and upwards, however, for the last major ascent of the day. Theres' a fairly indistinct path up to the trig point at the summit of Pen Cerrig-calch. In bad weather it's definitely worth taking a compass bearing to the trig point **B** 🕐 SO217223. In clear weather, the path through the bracken is visible rising up the spur. Beware of the false summit however, but once it begins to flatten out, a boggy path leads to a fairly visible cairn. From there it's a short walk to the trig point and a large cairn.

through a field. At the end, there's another gate and clearly displayed arrows that lead to Table Mountain. Walk north along this track.

Now, not to beat around the bush, this is the strenuous bit. There's a very long hike uphill that, from the start, will take just over an hour.

At the next stile, you'll see the words 'Table Mountain' carved into a wooden placard nailed to the stile. Hop over this and continue the slog straight uphill across the field. You'll see another stile at the top of that field and a lovely sign pointing right that says 'To mountain' (In this area, the signage, while excellent, is admirable in its brevity: 'to mountain', 'to road' etc.). Partly because you probably need a break already, it's worth wiping the sweat from your eyes and turning around to wonder at the view.

The distinctive Sugar Loaf, reminiscent of Roseberry Topping in North Yorkshire, stands to attention to the south east above all the surroundings. To the south, the jagged Llangatock Escarpment acts as barrier to the

Looking back to the ancient fort on Table Mountain

The 'shake holes', marked on the OS 1:25,000 map, refer to an inlier, an area of older rocks surrounded by younger rocks leaving holes in the ground. In this case, the mountain is Old Red Sandstone with an outcrop of limestone. Indeed, the name of the mountain means 'top of the limestone rock' in Welsh.

From the trig point, the full expanse of the mountain, cinched in the middle, opens out to the north. The next destination is the trig point at the top of the subsidiary mountain of Pen Allt-mawr, a highly distinctive peak with a broad shoulder that descends steeply to the north and east to link with the parent peak of Waun Fach far in the distance.

Seeing Pen Allt-mawr, and the clear and sweeping path, is an alluring prospect. In

View west towards the central Brecon Beacons

Remains of a quarry on the slopes of Tal Trwynau

bad weather, take a bearing to the lowest point where there is a pile of stones at **C** ⊙ SO210229. From here the path that skirts around the steep eastern slopes should be clear.

Trot along this path while admiring the desolate Black Mountains to the east. The trig point can't be seen until you're nearly upon it, so continue along the path to Pen Allt-mawr until you see it surrounded by rocks and a cairn shelter. From here, the views are stupendous, and you can see far into Wales in all directions. Also clearly visible is the next peak of the walk, Pen Twyn Glas.

The path descends steeply down a rock path to the col directly north. Take care to find the path which is slightly to the east side of the rocky shelter. Here we saw Welsh ponies grazing.

The soft ground makes for a pleasant stretch curving around to the indistinct summit of Pen Twyn Glas [**D** ⊙ SO213257], which is only marked by a couple of stones, not the huge cairns common in this area (it's a grassy summit, so

it would take some effort to drag them up). Before arriving at the summit there is a fork in the path. Take the right-hand path that leads east as opposed to north-east. And from here it is, mostly, downhill, back to Crickhowell, albeit with another nine kilometres to go.

Continue gently descending to a large cairn amidst a disused quarry and a jumble of rocks. From here the path descends quickly down to the left and the fence against the plantation. Vault the stile (!), and follow the finger post that reads 'To road'. Walk down the hill and along the rocky path following the signs to the road. There are signposts all along, but just before steep open hillside there's an arrow on a post that points steeply down the hill towards a great old oak tree – the next sign is partially hidden behind it. NOTE: the path here doesn't follow that marked on the OS map, but arrives at the road at **E** ⊙ SO234229. It doesn't seem like a temporary diversion.

The Red Lion, Llanbedr

From here, turn right onto the lane at the bridge, and follow it south and south-west. It's a pretty long jaunt back down this very quiet lane (we didn't see one car) back into Crickhowell. Fortunately, there's an excellent pub three kilometres down the lane into the picturesque village of Llanbedr, the kind of village that only has one postcode. And, quite honestly, by now you'll need a pint. To get to Llanbedr, take a left hand turn at **F** ⊗ SO234212.

Trig point on Pen Allt-mawr

The **T** **Red Lion** is just in front of the church of St Peter (Llanbedr means St Peter). It is an 11th-century church whose earliest recorded incumbent is John Wogan of Bulliston in 1495, according to a sign on the wall. One of the yew trees in the churchyard is reported on the church's website to be almost 3,000 years old.

The pub, a freehouse, is right by the church and distinguishable for its painted tan façade with red trim around the windows. There are a couple of delightful handpainted signs, one with typical Welsh wit, proclaiming it to be best pub in Llanbedr (of course, it's the only one). There was a little dog asleep on the flagstone hearth when we visited, a small bar, and a thoroughly homely feel to the place. The exposed stonework and a log fire invites you to stay even longer. There are

A large cairn on the descent to Crickhowell

Crickhowell bridge with the Bridge End Inn on the far side

several pumps, a couple dedicated to local beers including those from the Wye Brewery. On the notice board, a reproduction of Dylan Thomas's poem 'Do not go gentle into that good night' is pinned up. Whatever the original sentiment for putting up the poem, it does inspire one to stay for another pint. In another frame is the story of two aircraft of the US Eighth Army Air Force that crashed in to the mountainside just below the ridge you took down from Pen Twyn Glas on September 16, 1943 with the loss of all lives.

Those who are resisting another pint and the call of a lift or taxi back into Crickhowell are in for a 45-minute haul back into the town centre along a lane so take care of cars.

From the Red Lion, walk west up Maes Ffynnon and turn left at the end. Here it's a fair walk back around to the starting point, taking exactly the same route from where you turned off toward The Wern earlier in the day.

Back in Crickhowell, there are a couple of good pubs. The **2** **Bear Hotel** is a *Good Beer Guide* regular. It's a busy pub, popular for its excellent locally-sourced food, as it has been since the 15th century when it opened as a coaching inn. There is a mishmash of historical decorations from over the years, with some beautifully preserved wood panelling, wooden settles and two large fireplaces, roaring in winter. There's also some brilliant local art on the walls. There are two bars to stand at and enjoy a couple of guest ales, including from Rhymney Brewery on our visit. It's a grand place and still impresses more than 500 years later. Another good option for a drink is the **3** **Bridge End Inn**, especially on a warm day when you can sit outside and enjoy a drink by the river.

PUB INFORMATION

1 **RED LION**
Llanbedr, NP8 1SR
01874 730223
Opening hours: 7-11pm Tue-Fri; 1-11pm Sat; 12.30-10.30pm Sun

2 **BEAR HOTEL**
High Street, Crickhowell, NP8 1BW
01873 810408 · bearhotel.co.uk ·
Opening hours: 10-11 Mon-Sat; 11-10.30 Sun

TRY ALSO:

3 **BRIDGE END INN**
Bridge Street, Crickhowell, NP8 1AR
01873 810338 · thebridgeendinn.com·
Opening hours: 11-11; 12-11 Sun; 11-2.30am Fri & Sat

Cadair Idris

WALK 22

Cadair Idris, the giant, is an impressive sight from all angles. This vast mountain was carved out by mighty glacial forces during the last ice age, leaving a complex structure of cwms, moraines, scree and lakes. It has impressed local storytellers for hundreds of years and there are plenty of tales set upon the mountain. For the walker, there are a wide variety of ways to reach the 893-metre summit. This route carves along a little-used path that leads up the eastern ridge to the top Mynydd Moel before the final push to Cadair Idris summit. It returns down on the Pony Path, the most common way up the mountain, and then back into Dolgellau.

▶ **Start/finish:** Torrent Walk Hotel, Dolgellau

▶ **Duration:** 5–7hrs

▶ **Distance:** 11 miles (18km)

▶ **Ascent:** 3,323ft (1013m)

▶ **Fitness:**

▶ **Navigation:**

▶ **OS map:** Explorer OL23 *Cadair Idris & Llyn Tegid*

▶ **Key attractions:** Cymer Abbey, Talyllyn Railway

▶ **THE PUBS:** Torrent Walk Hotel, Dolgellau; George the Third Hotel, Penmaenpool

▶ **Timing tips:** There is still a fair walk to Dolgellau from the end of the Pony Path at Ty Nant – consider making a friend! Alternatively, you could start a much shortened route to Cadair Idris and back from this point, using the Ty Nant car park and walking up and down the Pony Path.

The summit of Mynydd Moel

It's a very long day out, with some mildly complicated navigation to gain the ridge. It can be made much easier, and shortened considerably, by parking at Ty Nant car park [SH698152] and walking up and down the Pony Path. Once back in Dolgellau, the pub of choice is the Torrent Walk Hotel. If you book ahead, you can combine a pub visit with a tour of Cader Ales brewery in the town. Also well worth visiting is George the Third Hotel, beautifully situated on the riverside in nearby Penmaenpool.

Dolgellau to Mynydd Moel

We're going to leave the pleasant market town of Dolgellau to the south-east, before climbing up to the eastern ridge of Cadair Idris. It's a reasonably simple start, but be warned that the paths up onto the ridge from where the road stops are subtle. It would be tricky if the cloud was down (in which case I'd recommend the Pony Path).

Our walk starts at the Torrent Walk Hotel, on Smithfield Street (there's a large paid-for car park by Dolgellau Rugby Club – a better option than the main car park just before it). From the pub, walk east along Arran

The Afon Arran tumbling through woodland

Council
Offices

Pen-y-
coed

Coll

-y-gwin

18

31

Clogwyn

Weirs

Pandy

Wenallt

Cemy

DOLGELLAU

Groeslw

A 494

Sch

Hospl

A

Fron-gôch

Tyddyn-
Ednyfed

102

Rhydwen

Brynrhug

Cairn

228

Bwlch-ôch

B

ichwydd

Nant y

Maes-côch

543

C

D

Llyn Gafr

833

E

363

Mynydd
Moel

I D R I S

ygadair

Llyn
Cau

CADER IDRIS

Road to cross the bridge over Afon Arran. Turn right immediately alongside the river past the cottages. Follow Penbrynglas onto Felin Uchaf until the road comes to an end and two paved paths split left and right. Turn right uphill and follow the path as it rises above the river and bends around to the left. At **A** SH734171, you'll hit a narrow lane. Turn right onto the road and walk along it as it bends sharply to the right, before continuing generally south towards the mountain. It's a quiet road, but there are a couple of blind corners to be wary of.

It's a pleasant stretch of road, and at various points, Cadair Idris flashes glimpses of its majesty. There are also waterfalls along this part of the river. Keep left at the fork in the road where there's a small sign on a tree marked to Tyn-sarn. You'll also pass Tyn-y-Bryn.

It gets tricky here. As the road comes to an end, follow the footpath sign and head through the gate towards the sheepfold. At the sheepfold, the path splits. Go through the gate on the left path that bends up to the left. It curves again to

the right. Follow the path until you reach crossroads at **B** SH748156 as the land flattens out. It's easy to miss so keep an eye on your grid reference. Turn right (south-west) onto this path and through the gate on the first wall. Hopefully, in clear weather, you'll see it weaving up towards the Mynydd Moel under the ridge. The path dips down and over a little stream before rising up again and over a wooden stile. The path goes up a little mound and flattens out again. At **C** SH743149, just before the path hits another wall, you'll see a small track that heads left and almost back on yourself up to the ridge at a small col. This path is not marked on the latest OS Explorer map (online, Jan 2017). But once on the ridge, there is a reasonably clear path. Looking up you'll see a wooden stile at **D** SH745145. As you'll see, there's a cliff down to your left into Gau Graig; a fence prevents you getting too close.

The path then weaves around the rocks and up, under the highest part of the ridgeline towards the sharpest looking part of the ridge, just before the path ascends

Looking up towards Mynydd Moel

On the Gau Graig ridge leading up to Mynydd Moel

steeply up to Mynydd Moel. You can relax now, the navigation gets markedly easier.

Once on the narrowest part of the ridge, the path hugs the fence, before clearly climbing up to the summit of Mynydd Moel. As it flattens out towards the top, there are a couple of low cairns to follow, particularly important where the path peters out. From here, and along the ridge to Cadair Idris, the views are unbelievable – this has to be one of the finest viewpoints in Wales. The peaks of northern Snowdonia, including Snowdon itself, can be clearly made out. To the south, you also realise what a mountainous place Wales is – the hills seem to go on forever. Over the cliff to the northeast is Llyn Arran, a small lake that feeds the river we've followed up from Dolgellau.

Mynydd Moel to Dolgellau

Now, you may want to cover your ears, for Cadair Idris is the hunting grounds of the spectral Hounds of Annwn, the Cŵn Annwn, and to anyone who hears them, death is coming and their soul will be dragged to the Otherworld. It is particularly on Halloween when the hound's owner, Gwyn ap Nudd, can be heard cheering them on during the Wild Hunt, a European folk myth in which ghostly, nocturnal huntsmen charge across the land in wild pursuit. Granted, you are more likely to hear the yaps of an overexcited Collie up here, but the barking of the hounds is also associated with the noise made by migrating geese.

Another well-known legend about Cadair Idris is that if you sleep alone on the mountain you'll awake either a poet or a madman. It comes from the time when bards would sleep on the mountains looking for inspiration. I'm not sure it's worth the risk, so we'll press on.

View from Gau Graig to Mynydd Moel

Ice-shattered rocks on Cadair Idris

If it is clear, you'll be able to see the summit of Cadair Idris from here, but it is further that it seems. Fog or no fog, there's a reasonably clear path now. Firstly, cross the stile at **E** ⊙ SH726136 and take the path down to the cliff top. We're describing the route in summer, but in winter all along here would be prone to cornices. The path largely follows the cliff edge (take care!). Just before the summit, there's a cairn that marks the top of the Fox's Path, the most direct route to the summit, but up some very steep and eroded scree. It looks daunting and dangerous, and few guides suggest the path.

Now for the final push to the top. It's a very rocky summit and you'll have to pick your way over the frost-shattered rocks to tap that summit trig point. Arriving from the direction we have, there's a surprisingly tangled summit over the other side, and that includes shelters of varying complexity, including a substantially maintained shelter with a roof (if you did want to spend the night and see if you awoke a poet or a madman). A little farther down to the left of the path you'll also see a fireplace that was once a summit cafe. Down to the south is Llyn Cau, the result of a cirque glacier that scooped out this cwm. This shape also gives rise to the mountain's name: Cadair Idris, or Idris's Chair. Idris

was, of course, a giant, a 7th-century prince who fought with the Irish here. The very summit is known as Penygader, or Penygadair, meaning chair or stronghold.

We now return along the Pony Path and you'll likely see more and more people. Be sure to start the descent in the right direction, picking out a path down the western slopes and past the fireplace. There are a couple of

The rocky approach to Cadair Idris

distinctive rocks called Pillow Lavas to pass. Stay away from the edge above Llyn y Gadair, especially on windy days (which is a lot of the time). The steep descent soon flattens out. There are a series of cairns to follow and a wide rocky path. The Pony Path leaves the cliff top at **F**  SH704131. Again, it is marked with a series of cairns and heads almost directly west, and then north-west to a fence at **G** SH691135. The Pony Path is known as such because of its use by ponies as beasts of burden to transport flour and butter from Llanfihangel y Pennant to the market at Dolgellau. By the Georgian era, tourists were already using the path to get to the summit.

LLyn Gwernan from the lane back to Dolgellau

We then start descending north and along a steep, but a clear path. You'll arrive at a stream and a gate in the wall. The Park Authority's website points out that the large patch of grass on your right, by the banks of the stream, is greener and contains broad-leaved plants, compared with the area we've just walked through that has fewer nutrients in the ground. The path descends further through a dry-stone wall and then into the first

George the Third Hotel on the Afon Mawddach

Bar at the Torrent Walk Hotel

trees we've seen for a while. Hop through the woodland, across a stone bridge and through a kissing gate. Keep an eye out for dippers on the stream here. You'll arrive out at Tŷ Nant farm. Turn left along the lane and down to the road.

Turn right on the road – it's another hour now back to Dolgellau. You'll pass the car park from where most people park to climb Cadair Idris. The road is very quiet, but take care all the same. You'll pass Llyn Gwernan on your right and a bar at the Gwernan Hotel. You'll then meet a T-junction at Rhydwen. Follow the road around to the left and then all the way into the town. When you get to the junction with Cader

Road, turn right and follow it right along into the centre of the town and then along Finsbury Square (passing Stryd Fawr on the left). To get to the Torrent Walk Hotel, turn left at the end of Finsbury Square into Smithfield Street. The hotel is just around the corner on the left. The **1 Torrent Walk Hotel**, a regular in the *Good Beer Guide*, is an 18th-century hotel. The main bar is a cosy spot with a large inglenook fireplace and wood burning stove. As you walk in, the pub's commitment to beer can be seen by the range of pump clips stuck to the beams above the room. There's always a good range of changing beers on across the pumps, many of them local beers. There are also ciders available. A part of the pub is set for refurbishment.

Also in Dolgellau, back to the west of town near the rugby club, is **3 Cader Ales brewery**. They run tours several times a week which cost £5 including tastings and a glass. You'll need to book in advance but it's well worth the visit.

In nearby Penmaenpool, a five-minute drive away, is another pub recommended in the *Good Beer Guide*, the **2 George the Third Hotel**. It dates way back to 1650 as an inn for the local boat-building industry. There are 11 rooms and a good-sized restaurant, plus two bars. The Dresser Bar and the Cellar Bar stock real ales, mostly from local breweries.

PUB INFORMATION

1 Torrent Walk Hotel
Smithfield Street, Dolgellau, LL40 1AA
01341 422858 • 🛏
Opening hours: 11–midnight

2 George the Third Hotel
Penmaenpool, LL40 1YD
01341 422525 • georgethethird.co.uk • 🛏
Opening hours: 11–11

TRY ALSO:

3 Cader Ales brewery
Unit 4, Marian Mawr Enterprise Park,
Dolgellau, LL40 1UU
07931 734655 • www.caderales.com
(Tours must be booked in advance)

INDEX

The following index covers the key towns, villages and other places visited in the walks, notable landmarks and landforms along the routes, the many special features throughout the book and all the recommended pubs.

Bear Hotel, Crickhowell

Buck Inn, Malham

The Grey Horse, Balerno

Grog & Gruel, Fort William

Tyn y Coed Inn, Capel Curig

Winking Owl, Aviemore

CREDITS AND ACKNOWLEDGEMENTS

Photo Credits

The author and publisher would like to thank all the pubs, hotels and others who have kindly contributed images for this book. All other photos are by Daniel Neilson except those listed below:

[Key: t = top; b = bottom; c = centre; l = left; r = right]

Front cover (b) Alan Novelli/Alamy Stock Photo, (t) Bob Steel; Back cover (b) Ed Daynes; p18 (b) & p24 (r) Matthew Dutson; p31 (t) luigi53/flickr, (b) Adam Bruderer/flickr; p34 Mark Croston/flickr; p36 (b) iknow-uk/flickr; p39 (b) sheppane2000/flickr; p40 (tl) Craig Loftus/flickr, (tr & b) Bob Steel; p48 (l) SLR Jester/flickr, (r) alljengi/flickr; p50 (b) Bob Steel; p56 (l) Bob Steel, (r) Mark Gilligan; p101, p102 (b), p105, p106 (b), p108 (tl, tr & b) Ed Daynes; p120 Andrew Bowden/flickr; p159 Phil Dolby/flickr (CC BY 2.0); p162 (b) Ed Loach/flickr (CC BY 2.0); p163 SNappa2006/flickr (CC BY 2.0); p184 (l) Andrew/flickr (CC BY 2.0); p176 (t & b) Andrew Bowden/flickr (CC BY-SA 2.0); p164 afcone/flickr (CC BY-ND 2.0).

Map Credits

Ordnance Survey mapping provided by: National Map Centre, Hatfield.
All base mapping © Crown Copyright (2013–2017). All rights reserved. Licence Number 100031961.
Contains OS data © Crown copyright and database right (2013).

Author's Acknowledgements

I'd like to thank the great team at CAMRA books, in particular Julie, Simon and Katie for their support and belief in the idea. The local CAMRA branches were, of course, invaluable at recommending pubs, walks and many have been enthusiastic in their support. Research for the Lake District walks was helped greatly by the service at Co-wheels Car Club*, the team at **golakes.com** and by Virgin Trains**. On a more personal note, I'd like to thank my wife Cat, for understanding when I jumped in a car every weekend to go do something cool. And finally, to my Mum Judy, whose unerring support has meant I can go off and do projects like this one.

Publisher's Acknowledgements

The publisher would like to thank all of the licensees and others who kindly contributed photographs to this book. Also, our thanks to Matt Robin at the National Map Centre for his invaluable advice and help sourcing mapping for all of the walks. Finally, thanks to all the local CAMRA branches who recommended pubs to feature in the walks.

*Co-wheels Car Club is a 'pay by the hour' car club with a car stationed at Oxenholme and many other locations. You can access a car 24 hours a day, without the cost and hassle of owning one (**co-wheels.org.uk**).
** Virgin Trains travel between London Euston and Oxenholme Lake District in under three hours and depart every hour (**virgintrains.co.uk**).

BOOKS FOR BEER LOVERS

CAMRA Books, the publishing arm of the Campaign for Real Ale, is the leading publisher of books on beer and pubs. Key titles include:

GOOD BEER GUIDE 2017

Editor: Roger Protz

CAMRA's *Good Beer Guide* is fully revised and updated each year and features pubs across the United Kingdom that serve the best real ale. Now in its 44th edition, this pub guide is completely independent with listings based entirely on nomination and evaluation by CAMRA members. This means you can be sure that every one of the 4,500 pubs deserves their place, plus they all come recommended by people who know a thing or two about good beer.

£15.99   ISBN 978-1-85249-335-6

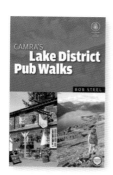

LAKE DISTRICT PUB WALKS

Bob Steel

A guide to some of the best pubs and best walking in the Lake District, this guide features 30 walks of varying lengths, aimed at both the casual walker and more serious hiker, and explores some of the region's fascinating cultural heritage and local attractions. Each route has been chosen for its inspiring landscape, historic interest and its beer. Full-colour Ordnance Survey maps and detailed route information, alongside pub listings with opening hours and details of draught beers, make this book the essential guide for anyone wanting a taste of the Lakes.

£9.99   ISBN 978-1-85249-271-7

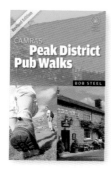

PEAK DISTRICT PUB WALKS

Bob Steel

A practical pocket-sized traveller's guide to some of the best pubs and best walking in the Peak District. This book features 25 walks, as well as cycle routes and local attractions, helping you see the best of Britain's oldest National Park while never straying too far from a decent pint. Each route has been selected for its inspiring landscape, historical interest and welcoming pubs.

£9.99   ISBN 978-1-85249-246-5

YORKSHIRE PUB WALKS

Bob Steel

This is a pocket-sized, traveller's guide to some of the best walking and finest pubs in Yorkshire. The walks are grouped geographically and explore some of the region's fascinating historical and literary heritage as well as its thriving brewing scene. The book contains essential information about local transport and accommodation. The walks include: Settle and Upper Ribblesdale; Whitby to Robin Hood's Bay; Brontë country: Haworth and Ponden; Sheffield: Kelham Island and the 'valley of beer' and Hull's old town: a fishy trail. The book covers towns and cities as well as rural areas, i.e. Beverley; Hull; Leeds; Sheffield and York.

£9.99   ISBN 978-1-85249-329-5

SOUTH EAST PUB WALKS

Bob Steel

A practical pocket-sized guide to some of the best pubs and best walking in the South East. The guide features 30 walks of varying lengths, all accessible by public transport and aimed at both the casual walker and more serious hiker. Each route has been selected for its varied landscape, and its beer - with the walks taking you on a tour of the best real-ale pubs the area has to offer.

£9.99   ISBN 978-1-85249-287-8

LONDON PUB WALKS

Bob Steel

CAMRA's pocket-size walking guide to London is back. This fully redesigned third edition is packed with updated, new pubs and new routes that take full advantage of London's public transport network. With 30 walks around more than 200 pubs, CAMRA's *London Pub Walks* enables you to explore the entire city while never being far from a decent pint.

£11.99   ISBN 978-1-85249-336-3

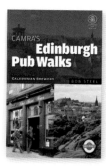

EDINBURGH PUB WALKS

Bob Steel

CAMRA's *Edinburgh Pub Walks* has everything you need to know to explore the many faces of Scotland's capital city, while never straying too far from a decent pint. It offers a guide to some of the best pubs in Edinburgh and the surrounding area and features 25 town, country and coastal walks all accessible by public transport from the heart of the city. Each pub has been chosen for its quality ale, its location and its architectural heritage. Fully illustrated throughout, high-quality street-level mapping helps you navigate easily and join up trails for longer walks.

£9.99   ISBN 978-1-85249-274-8

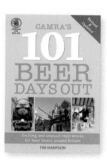

101 BEER DAYS OUT

Tim Hampson

Revised and updated for 2015, *101 Beer Days Out* is the perfect handbook for the beer tourist wanting to explore beer, pubs and brewing in the UK. From brewery tours to rail-ale trails, beer festivals to hop farms, brewing courses to historic pubs, Britain has a huge variety of beer experiences to explore and enjoy. *101 Beer Days Out* is ordered geographically, so you can easily find a beer day out wherever you are in Britain, and includes full visitor information, maps and colour photography, with detailed information on opening hours, local landmarks and public transport links to make planning any excursion quick and easy.

£12.99   ISBN 978-1-85249-328-8

SO YOU WANT TO BE A BEER EXPERT?

Jeff Evans

More people than ever are searching for an understanding of what makes a great beer, and this book meets that demand by presenting a hands-on course in beer appreciation, with sections on understanding the beer styles of the world, beer flavours, how beer is made, the ingredients, and more. Uniquely, *So You Want to Be a Beer Expert?* doesn't just relate the facts, but helps readers reach conclusions for themselves. Key to this are the interactive tastings that show readers, through their own taste-buds, what beer is all about. CAMRA's *So You Want to Be a Beer Expert?* is the ideal book, for anyone who wants to further their knowledge and enjoyment of beer.

£12.99   ISBN 978-1-85249-322-6

Order these and other CAMRA books online at **www.camra.org.uk/books**, ask at your local bookstore, or contact: CAMRA, 230 Hatfield Road, St Albans, AL1 4LW. Telephone 01727 867201.

JOIN THE CAMPAIGN!

CAMRA, the Campaign for Real Ale, is an independent not-for-profit, volunteer-led consumer group. We promote good-quality real ale and pubs, as well as lobbying government to champion drinkers' rights and protect local pubs as centres of community life.

CAMRA has over 185,000 members from all ages and backgrounds, brought together by a common belief in the issues that CAMRA deals with and their love of good-quality British beer. From just £25 a year – that's less than a pint a month – you can join CAMRA and enjoy the following benefits:

- A monthly colour newspaper (*What's Brewing*) and award-winning quarterly magazine (*BEER*) containing news and features about beer, pubs and brewing.

- Free or reduced entry to over 200 national, regional and local beer festivals.

- Money off many of our publications including the *Good Beer Guide* and the *Good Bottled Beer Guide*.

- A 10% discount on all holidays booked with Cottages.com and Hoseason's, a 10% discount with Beer Hawk, plus much more.

- £20 worth of J D Wetherspoon real ale vouchers* (40 × 50 pence off a pint).

- Discounts in thousands of pubs across the UK through the CAMRA Real Ale Discount Scheme.

- 15 months membership for the price of 12 for new members paying by Direct Debit**

For more details about member benefits please visit **www.camra.org.uk/benefits**

If you feel passionately about your pint and about pubs, join us by visiting **www.camra.org.uk/join** or calling **01727 798 440**

For the latest campaigning news and to get involved in CAMRA's campaigns visit **www.camra.org.uk/campaigns**

*Joint members receive £20 worth of J D Wetherspoon vouchers to share.
15 months membership for the price of 12 is only available the first time a member pays by Direct Debit. **NOTE: Membership prices and benefits are subject to change.